Deception To The Nth Degree

A Story Of How To Become Victorious Over Deception

Mary Taylor

Table of Contents

Chapter	Description	Page
	Introduction	5
1	Childhood	6
2	A Baby with A Baby	30
3	Pursuing My Dreams	37
4	Love in All the Wrong Places	44
5	Drugs	61
6	The Betrayals	84
7	Meeting God near The Edge	99
8	Ronnie	108
9	Starting Over	130
10	Deliverance, Restoration and Promotion	141
Bibliography		196

This book is a work of non-fiction. It is an honest and accurate account of my life, insofar as I have been able to remember and research. However, the names have been changed to protect their identities. They are identified in the book by fictitious names.
Copyright ©2006 by Mary Taylor
All rights reserved.

ISBN: 978-0-6151-7747-2

This book is first dedicated to God, without Him, this would have never happened. Secondly, my daughter, Michelle, little do you know that, with God's prompting, you have kept me going for such a time as this. Thirdly, to my sister Norvelle and my sister in Christ Dianne, thanks for your editing help. And last but not the least, the rest of my family thanks for the challenges and experiences. I love you all.

Introduction

I was taken by deception to the Nth degree. What is deception? Deception can be anything from a little "twist" of the truth to total dishonesty. Deception is believing something that has just a little error, but if that error isn't corrected, it will progressively lead us into total destruction.

For example: As a pilot flies an airplane he is always making corrections to stay on course. If he would just accept a fraction of an error in his flight plan, he would be totally off course and endangering his life and the lives of his passengers. When we accept that little "twist"; it makes us more and more vulnerable to other areas of deception. I'm going to tell you a story about how self-deception led me into a life of lies, drugs, alcohol, and sex.

This is my public acknowledgement of what happened and the forgiving process I had to undergo to forgive myself and the persons involved in the deceptions to become victorious. I must admit, writing this book was an awfully humbling experience.

Chapter 1

Childhood

I am the tenth of the twelve children of Nora Bell and Roland Lee Byars, born as Mary Frances Byars on March 5th 1957. I was born when our family lived at 230 N. California Ave, in Chicago, IL. We lived in a two bedroom, front half, of a split apartment. Seven children lived in this apartment, my four brothers and three of my older sisters. My parent and I slept on a pull out/couch bed in the living room. (Side Bar: Which meant, I was in the bed with them during the conception of my younger sisters and if you are wondering, I did not see my parents have sex.) One of my earliest memories, as a toddler, was one day upon awaking, I was confronted by the eyes of a cat sitting on the mantel above our fireplace. We did not own a cat. He had entered in through an open window. Mama took a broom and chased him out.

My sisters Rhoda and Natalie informed me, that when I was a baby, my brother Chuck would scream over my crib and awaken me. They informed me that this behavior caused me to be very nervous. He was young and did not know how to ward off teasing that siblings do to one another and would scream at whomever was teasing him. This time, he was being teased about his baby sister having a round yellow head like his. The rule of thumb was not to roughhouse or tease one another when the baby was napping. He couldn't take the heat and would scream.

I also fell down our front stairs as a toddler. I really injured myself because I started to bleed from my vagina. It was summer and back then, our front door was always open. The kids were going in and out. I followed the kids into the hallway. I fell, because I did not know how to walk down the stairs. My mother laid me on the couch to examine me; my aunt Georgia was also there and I remembered feeling embarrassed having her see me. Upon going to the hospital, my mother was told that my hymen was ruptured from the fall.

My father would fight my mother, this is an incident that shaped my character. My father was a gambler. On this particular night, he demanded "his" money back that he had given her to pay the bills. She refused. She was combing my sister's hair and I was standing beside her. He took her purse from her, took the money out, and threw the purse back at her, missing her and hitting me on the forehead which produced a cut. (Notice, she had to keep her purse with her)

My mom made a butterfly bandage to close the cut. It seemed that she was always doctoring on us. We had no health insurance or money. It was by necessity and through the grace of God that she learned a few medical tricks and having older children to practice her craft on. I remember thinking that she had a cure for everything.

My dad felt so bad after seeing that he had hurt one of his children, that he gave the money back and did not go out to gamble that night.

As I got older, I guess I was allowed, on occasion, to play, with my sisters, in the vacant lot (our playground) which was two doors down from our apartment. My only knowledge of this is a picture of me running through the lot.

Another past-time activity for me was to sit under the dining room table and bang on a Quaker Oatmeal Box as a drum.

The memories I have, of this apartment, are of a dark place. I don't know if it was dark or that my memory is not clear on the events because I was very young.

I was told that Mama became ill shortly after I was born and went into the hospital for an extended period of time. I know now that she had pneumonia. This was my first experience with the feeling of rejection/abandonment. My sister Rhoda, being the eldest at the time (seventeen years old) cared for me during her absence. The neighbors thought that I was her child. When Mama returned from the hospital, my sister got married and moved to Florida. I really missed her. I thought she was my mother too. My sister Rhoda, was considered pretty. She was what black people would call "light skinned". She had very fine features too. I was told that when I would see women on TV, I would cry out for her, thinking that these women, who happen to be white, were my sister. I guess this was the second feeling of rejection and abandonment.

Our landlord, Leonard Watts; who looked like a white man, would come to visit all the time. I thought he was family. I later learned that he was also a friend. I know you are wondering, what's with the white people analogy? As a kid I had a hard time distinguishing white from black. My mother was very light skinned and she was my barometer for who was white or black. I remember telling her that my teacher was black. When she came to school for a parent teacher conference, she discovered that the teacher was white. I didn't know! She was the same color as my mother! So, as you can tell, I was confused about color.

My younger sisters, Marsha and Jackie were also born when we lived in the apartment on California as stated before I was in the bed with my parents when they were created but did not witness it. (emphasized because my sisters thought I meant I saw my parents have sex.)

My older brother Dennis went to a juvenile detention facility for robbery. On Sunday's Mama would pack a picnic basket and the entire family would go to St Charles, IL to visit him. Mama wrote a very beautiful letter to him that was published in the St Charles newspaper and aided in his release. We had a picture of him holding my baby sister Jackie upon his arrival home.

My sister Rhoda, who went to Florida, returned with a baby, my nephew Donald. She moved back in with us. She then started dating a guy name Isaiah who was called Chicken. When Chicken would come to visit her and would sit on the couch, I would get out of the rocking chair I was in and try to push him off the couch. He would get up and I would then sit on the couch and rock and suck my thumb. He would then try to sit in the rocker I just relinquished and I would start to cry again until he got up. Their visitation was then limited to the kitchen or on the front porch. My sister did not take heed to my discernment of this man and she married him anyway. Rhoda abandoned me again, when she married Chicken. Later we would laugh about the rocker and couch scenario. She would even say, that my actions had to be a sign from God and that she should have heeded. We all know that hind sight is 20/20.

Our family then moved to 4053 W Gladys. This neighborhood was mixed when we moved in, there were several white families on the block. It appeared as if they moved out over night. One white woman, who lived next door to us, would give us hard candy, lollipops, that made us sick. The next time she gave us candy, we threw it away.

The apartment on Gladys had three-bedrooms with a living room, dining room and kitchen. It also had one and a half baths. Eight children and two adults lived in this apartment. This place seemed huge, I guess because I was little. It had walk-in closets big enough, that we set up, what we called, a club house in one of them.

Both of my parents worked full-time jobs. Mama would come home from work and cook dinner. My younger sisters and I would ask if we could wash dishes. We were not tall enough yet. I was in second grade, my sister Marsha was in first grade and Jackie was in kindergarten. We stood on chairs to help, we thought, my older sisters wash dishes. My mother would say, "you are not going to always want to do this". We liked playing with the bubbles. We washed dishes with tide and bleach. My parents didn't buy dishwashing liquid.

Every Friday, my father would bring home shrimp for my mother to cook. This was a treat for us. He still practiced the, Catholic church's, ritual of fish/no meat, on Friday. Mama and my two older sisters, Natalie and Paula, would de-vein, batter and fry the shrimp. Mama made her own special cocktail sauce too.

My older sisters, Enid, Rhoda, and Martha, their husbands and children would visit every weekend. In our minds, we thought we were having a party. When we all got together, it was like having a party.

My father bought a Grand Prix while we lived on Gladys. The kids wanted to go for a ride in his new car. One Friday my sisters and I convinced him to take us to the drive-in. Back in the day, one had to park next to a pole that had speakers with wires attached to it. You would have to take the speaker, which had a clip on it, and slide the clip onto your window to hear the movie.(As time went on, the drive-in progressed to tuning your radio to a particular frequency/channel to pick up the sound). We bought popcorn and spilled it on the floor of daddy's new car. He made us clean it up, of course, and we ate the popcorn too. Remember, it wasn't dirty, the car was new. Now that's kid's logic.

I learned a lot about life on Gladys Ave. I went to Edward C. Delano, (Delano, for short) grade school. I even learned about sex in kindergarten. I allowed a little boy to touch me. I remember the teacher getting upset by this and spanking me; this was my first indication that sex was wrong or boys should not touch girls. Also note: the teacher would spank students who misbehaved. The message I heard at home was don't have sex with boys because you would become pregnant. I deceived myself into thinking, at a young age, that it was then ok to have sex with girls. There was a female neighbor in our building that I allowed to touch me. My self-deceit/justification allowed me to continue this wrongful act. I knew it was wrong but it felt good. We would hide under the porch and rub against each other. We were caught by a guy who lived next door. She and I found another place that was not so public. The girl and her family moved and another family moved in.

Vanessa was the name of one of the girls who moved in. She was a chunky girl with breasts. I did not develop breasts until high school, (at least, what I would call breasts). Vanessa was a very sexually active child. When we would go up to her apartment, so we could walk to school together, her mom would be naked. Her mom was a big woman too. My guess would be around 300 pounds. I would not walk around naked if I was that big. But I'm not her. I guess she had a healthy self image of her body because she did not care if we saw her. Or, maybe she was just a dirty old lady. Vanessa had older sisters that were also very sexually active and I think they or someone may have abused her. Vanessa taught me some things about sex too. We use to spend time together when her mom and sisters were not at home. I knew these things were wrong but I did them anyway. In life we always have to make moral choices. I would justify the fact that she could not get me pregnant. But the fact that I kept it a secret was a dead give away that what I was doing was wrong.

My sister Natalie was raped in the hallway of our apartment building coming home from school; this was of course, really bad for all of us. This changed my life because now when I ran through the alleys and gangways I had to be aware of my surroundings. We had to accompany each other when going to the store, school, or just hanging outside. This rape helped me to also justify my behavior with Vanessa. Little did I know, at the time, that girls could also rape girls.

While playing in our back yard, we noticed one of our neighbors, a white man, would dance naked in his bathroom window while we were outside or looking out of our bedroom window. He would wiggle and do lewd things in front of us. We would tell Mama about it but she never caught him because when we would leave the window to get her, the man would hide. But one day, while he was doing his dance, I kept him occupied while I sent one of my little sisters in to get Mama. When she caught him, she really gave him a piece of her mind.

I don't know why she didn't call the police. With all of these things happening in the neighborhood, Mama gave us a curfew. We had to be in the house when the street lights came on. We called this "Opie Taylor" time. That was the time the character named Opie Taylor, had to come into the house on the series Andy Griffin.

We were not allowed to use the telephone to call our friends, so I devised a way for us to communicate via our bedroom window. Vanessa would send a string down from her window with a note attached. I would retrieve the note and write my response and she would pull it back up to her apartment. We could do this for hours until Mama came into the room to check if we were in bed, or my older sisters came in to go to bed. All five girls slept in one room. In this room there were three twin beds and one crib. My brothers slept in the other bedroom. I remember sneaking into their room and looking at pictures they had taken of naked girls. The Polaroid instamatic camera was new on the market. The instamatic made nude pictures more accessible because a person did not have to send the film to be developed. My brothers had an abundance of them.

A toy I enjoyed playing with was my oldest brother's, Roland, "visible" man. He was taking biology or anatomy, and the visible man could be taken apart and all of the human organs could be removed. It was like a 3-D puzzle. I enjoyed playing with the brain and the bones. I learned about anatomy from the visible man.

My oldest brother Roland, whom we called Bug, went into the army and was discharged because he was gay. This next incident explains the first, but I did not pay much attention to it at the time. My oldest brother was put out of our apartment. My father came home one night and said that someone told him that my brother was a "fag", so my father threw him out. My brother was named after my father. Bug would come to visit when my dad was not at home. He taught my older sisters how to apply make-up. I was much older when I finally started to see that he was gay. As a matter of fact, he moved in with Rhoda and Chicken and her two kids after daddy threw him out.

Rhoda would return, occasionally, to our apartment, with her kids. Chicken beat her. She stayed with that man and put up with him treating her like crap for over twenty years. She finally divorced him but he remained in her life until he died. Her children would invite him to family gatherings. Rhoda currently has rheumatoid arthritis and heart problems. I feel that her arthritis/illnesses are caused by the unresolved anger and resentment toward him and anyone else that hurt her.

As a child in grade school, I also learned how to be independent and the art of persuasion. I organized a club and collected dues. The club put on a talent show and charged admission. We also sold Popsicles made from Kool-Aid. To make the ghetto popsicles: make the Kool-Aid, pour into ice cube trays, cover with plastic wrap, and stick tooth picks into the plastic wrap. I think we sold each cube for 1 or 2 cents. We used the dues and money raised to go on outings and buy supplies. One day we wanted to have a picnic at a park further away from our apartment/ neighborhood. The neighborhood kids, in the club, did not want to ride the bus. I did not know how to take the bus because my parents did not allow us to venture out from in front of the house nor beyond the neighborhood. It was the summertime and, our parents were at work. I persuaded a Pastor, that lived several houses away from us, to give us a ride, if we paid for his gas and fed him. He transported us to the park and we had a good time. We rode the swings and merry-go-round and even played baseball. As I look back on this I am amazed how I was able to accomplish this as a child.

We could have gotten into a lot of trouble right in the neighborhood. The club decided to do something positive instead.

My little sisters and I transferred from Delano School to Melody, I think the school boundaries changed or they stopped having classes for children in fifth grade and below. My older sisters graduated from Delano and went to Marshall High School.

While living on Gladys, I also learned how to sing. My sister Natalie taught us how to harmonize. If we did not sing our parts correctly or didn't pay attention, she would hit us. Parts were then learned very fast. Singing was a frequent activity around the house. That was one thing we could do together. My sister Paula registered us for a talent show. We practiced, auditioned, and were selected out of a large group of acts. When it came time to perform, during a dress rehearsal, Marsha and I were afraid and cried. Paula then recruited her friends to make up a dance routine and danced in our place in the talent show.

My first encounter with religion, was my sisters Paula and Natalie going to catechism. I could not wait until I was old enough to participate but my mother stopped attending church. I was very disappointed. We were not practicing Catholics. Our family did not go to church every Sunday, especially after Mama was introduced to birth control by her adult daughters. Mama started taking birth control and stopped going to church. That's my take on it. I had such great respect for the nuns and priests. I wanted to be a nun. Mama told me, "you will not be able to have sex". At this time, I was in grade school, and having sex was not something I knew much about except the encounters I had with girls and letting a few boys touch me. If she had known, she should have jumped at the opportunity to stop her daughter from having sex, or so I thought.

My brother Chuck, that yelled over my crib when I was a baby, went to Vietnam. He was seriously injured. He still has shrapnel in his lungs, arms, and legs. Before he went to Vietnam, he got married to a girl that lived next door to us on Gladys. My other brothers tried to warn him not to marry the girl because she was a loose woman. One day they had a fight and she stabbed him and he came to our apartment bleeding and Mama took him to the hospital. This same woman tried to teach me how to smoke cigarettes but I was not interested. When Chuck returned from Vietnam he drank a lot. His wife's sister would tell me how she would let her niece feel her up, stroke her genitals. I later realized that this was sexual abuse. Things like this happened frequently in the neighborhood and family.

There was always something happening in our family. My brother Dennis broke his first wife's, nose while fighting her in our apartment. Mama tried to tell this girl not to marry him but she did not listen. They have a son who they named Dennis. They eventually got a divorce and he married a woman named Lestine. We use to tease her about her name and called her Listerine, like the mouth wash. My mother also told her not to marry Dennis but she did not listen either. He would also fight her. They had two children together. They did pretty well for themselves financially, with Dennis hustling and Lestine working. Dennis got into drugs, he and the youngest of my four brothers, Norris. They had nice jobs and had plenty of clothes, cars, and anything they wanted, but they were doing illegal activity to obtain their wealth. They were stealing from the delivery truck that belonged to their employer and selling the merchandise. At the time this was happening I was not aware. I learned about most of their dealings when I became older, 7th, 8th, or 9th grade. That's not that old but I paid attention to Mama telling my older sisters about these incidents. One never knows what their children hear them say. We must be mindful of that.

While attending Melody Grammar School I learned many things. I developed the artistic side of my personality. I learned to draw and to make crafts. Mama was very artistic too. She would make 3-D pictures, from the Styrofoam containers that meat is packed in. One of her jobs was to teach arts and crafts at a community center.

When Dr King and President Kennedy were killed, I was attending Melody Grammar School. I remember crying when Kennedy was shot. When Dr. King was shot it seemed that everybody in our neighborhood started looting. There was a different kind of sadness about King's death. Our attention became focused on staying safe and not on grieving him. There was a rumor at school that the Black Panthers were coming to the school (none of us knew any better and we called them the Black Pampers, the things kids say.) We were released from school so the white teachers could leave the neighborhood safely.

During the looting, my brothers stole shoes and other items that they could not bring home. If you didn't earn it, it was not coming into my parents home. White people that we saw everyday were beaten by people they knew. This was senseless, violence and destruction. Many businesses were burned. The business district of our neighborhood never recover from this event.

The big Chicago snow of 1967, what a memory! The snow was very deep, it was over the roofs of cars. Schools were closed, of course. Delivery trucks had a hard time delivering to the stores, many stores ran out of supplies. We would go outside, get soaked from playing in the snow and then return to the apartment to warm up. This was fun to us. Playing in snow is no longer a desire, I only like looking at it. Occasionally, if I'm dressed properly, and it's not below freezing, I get the same feeling I experienced as a child, while walking through snow.

One summer, I witnessed a little girl being struck by a taxicab. When the cab made contact with her, it dragged her several feet. Her face was disfigured and she was never the same. Prior to the accident, she was a pretty little girl. Her family sued the cab company.

As stated earlier, while living in the apartment on Gladys, both my parents worked. Mama started saving to buy a house. My sister Rhoda helped her and Mama allowed her to move into the first floor apartment on 642 N Christiana Ave. We were so happy to have a place of our own. We had a large back yard. My father poured concrete for a patio. We bar-be-qued on most summer holidays. We had a full basement and my father remodeled it into a family room. Sometimes when we had company, we would entertain in the basement instead of upstairs. I remember before the basement was remodeled, us kids wanted to have a party. We cleaned up the basement and painted the walls and floor. Rhoda drew cartoon characters on the walls.

Four children and 2 adults moved into the 2nd floor apartment on Christiana. My brother Chuck, who went to Vietnam, lived with us for a while. He would sit on the front porch, drink alcohol and chase the boys away. We girls did not like that. Mama would also get after him about sitting on the front porch and drinking until he passed out.

When we moved to Christiana, I attended Morton Upper Grade Center and Jackie and Marsha attended Morris elementary school. While on Christiana, we lived a block away from Mama's sister Naomi. I really liked her. She was a loving person but her husband was abusive and tried to alienate her from her family. If I had a problem I would visit and talk with her. She raised my cousin Wendy, her granddaughter. I thought Wendy was cute. She had what we called good hair and she was hairy. She even had hair on her stomach. Now, you may be wondering, how did I know that? Midriff tops were the fashion craze at this time. But I was also attracted to her.

On my twelfth birthday she accompanied me, via the bus, to downtown Chicago, we saw a movie and ate at a Chinese food restaurant. This was my first trip on a bus without Mama. Wendy was like an only child, living with her grandmother. I heard that Wendy's stepfather abused her and that was why she stayed with her grandmother. She has brothers and sisters but she was the only one that stayed with my aunt Naomi. Wendy got all the new stuff, clothes, bikes, and even a motorized mini-bike. She would take me for rides on her bike, for I could not ride a bike. I fell off while learning and did not try again. There are very few things I have given up on and that's one of them. As a child I would put forth effort and a lot of time, then give up. I don't give up anymore.

The neighborhood kids would get together and go for bike rides and I would accompany them riding on the back of someone's bike. I was not going to let a small thing like me not riding a bike prevent me from going. We had a ball. We went into neighborhoods that we would never go alone. We were also chased out too. It was exciting! It's amazing how we banded together to do things that were not destructive. I was always a ring leader in arranging these events, even though I could not ride a bike.

While at Morton, I gained confidence in academics. I participated in a group teaching environment where three different classes were combined and taught by three different teachers. We had a homeroom teacher but we spent most of the time in the lunchroom with the other two classes. This was the only room that could accommodate three classes. I performed very well in science and fell in love with my science teacher. I kept in contact with him after I graduated from High School. Mr. Perna, Mrs. Baranowski, and Mr. Schaffer were the three individuals who made an impact on my academic life.

Our school participated in a program called Project Wing Spread. The concept was to take inner city students and swap them with students from a suburban school to see how their lives are affected by the experience. Our school swapped with Morton Grove Grade School and we thought the school was a college. It was huge. It had everything, even video games in the lunchroom. The community/students were Jewish. It was an eye opener for all involved. We as a group went to, "Gladys' restaurant", a soul food restaurant, for lunch. We had fried chicken, that was the safest thing to order because our guest were Jewish. After the program some of the students stayed in contact. One of the girls I got to know, asked if I could spend the night at her house. Bad idea, if one is not an immediate family member. Mama, of course, said "No!" and then added, "Those people are freaky and I don't want them trying to do something to you!" Little did she know, I had already been freaked.

Chapter 2

A Baby with a Baby

I graduated from Morton and went to Rezin Orr High School. I attended my freshman year at the old Orr HS, located on Keeler Ave. I met a guy at school that wore a big "Angela Davis" afro. I thought he was handsome and so did he along with many other girls. He was at least six feet tall and chocolate brown. I introduced myself to him; he said his name was Sly. We went to the, Valentines Day dance, but not together. I went with my nephew Donald. Jonathan, known as Sly, taught me how to bop, a stepping dance. It was love at first sight/step. He invited me back to his parent's apartment. I went with my nephew in tow. Jonathan and I went to his bedroom and attempted to have sex. I was a virgin at that time and I thought that he was entering the wrong orifice. We did not consummate the relationship that night. But the next day we played hooky. We consummated the relationship then. I was hooked. I went to see him daily instead of going to school. The school contacted my home; luckily for me, my sister, Natalie was at home and intercepted the call. She confronted me and I told her that I would return to school.

I learned many things at Jonathan's house besides sex. I also learned how to get high. His sister Monica, taught me to smoke marijuana. I did not enjoy it because it burned my throat. Jonathan smoked cigarettes and marijuana and took acid. I tried to tell him that drugs could deform his children and mind. Little did I know that he was also using heroine. I became pregnant, it was inevitable, with all the sex we were having. I spoke of marriage and moving together but we were both just kids.

Madea, a neighbor that lived across the street, was having a party. We were invited but Mama would not allow us to attend because of the kind of people she said they were. In my mind, we were no different, the same thing that happened in their house happened in ours but Mama didn't know about it. I'm sure that Madea did not want her girls having sex, and using and selling drugs too. We did not sell drugs, so maybe that's what Mama meant. My boyfriend at the time, Jonathan, went to the party. My sister Marsha and I went to our basement and started playing records and put the speakers to the window. The next thing we knew, all the people from their party was coming to our house. I was only trying to get one person to come, my boyfriend Jonathan. See how deception can lead you into something you really don't want. Mama was furious with me and threw everyone out.

Some days later my Mama asked me if I was pregnant and I told her that I couldn't be! "I hadn't done anything to become pregnant". I informed my sister Paula, that I was pregnant and she told me to tell Mama. Before I told Mama, I found a school that allowed pregnant teens to attend. I did not want to drop out, like some of my older sisters who became pregnant while in school. I found the Family Living Center, located on Hoyne and Roosevelt Rd. I made an appointment and told Mama I was pregnant. She started to cry, I know she probably wished she had encouraged me to be a nun. She accompanied me to my first doctor's appointment to confirm my pregnancy. The appointment was at the health department. We called the building the "golden dome".

The Golden dome, was a beautiful building located in the middle of Garfield park. It had ballrooms, a swimming pool, and other facilities. The main dome was a golden color.

I had never been to a gynecologist prior to becoming pregnant. I was too young, and I had no need for one. I did not know what to expect and Mama did not inform me. I went into the doctor's office and was told to remove my clothes, sit on the table, put my legs in the stir-ups, and then scoot down to the edge of the table. I did what I was told. The doctor took the cold medal speculum and inserted it into my vagina. I screamed and started crying and begged her to take it out, I even told her that I would never do it/have sex again. She reassured me that I was a good girl and tried to calm me. Upon completion of the exam, I re-entered the waiting area with a tear stained face and embarrassed about how I behaved. I noticed that the doctor's office only had a door and no ceiling, so the conversation I had with the doctor could have been heard by anyone in the waiting area. But Mama never said a word about hearing me.

Mama escorted me to the appointment I scheduled at the Family Living Center's school. The first school we visited was one that did not focused on academics. I was informed of another location that focused on academics on Hoyne Ave. and Roosevelt Rd. The summer after my freshman year ended I enrolled at that location. I delivered my daughter, on Dec 7th 1972; I continued attending the school until the summer of 1973. My classmates from Orr High School thought I had dropped out.

While I was attending Family Living Center, Jonathan was kicked out of Orr because of drugs and attendance. He started attending an alternative school.

I returned to the New Rezin Orr in the fall of 1973. The new building was built on Pulaski Rd. and Chicago Ave. The school had four separate buildings connected to one central section. The gym was accessed by going through a tunnel. It was the nicest school in the area. We also had a choir and band room. My younger sister, Marsha, and I were in the choir. We were chosen to sing in an ensemble group and competed on the city level. Our choir won all-city awards on several occasions. The ensemble would go to the music teacher's, Mrs. Wright, home for rehearsals. Mrs. Bessie Wright sang opera at one time in her life and she was a great music teacher. Her children were also very talented. I graduated from Orr with the 1974 class. I was supposed to graduate in 1975. Everyone thought that when I returned I would be behind but I graduated before the freshmen I started with. My GPA was over 3.5 too, an ego boasting accomplishments. Proverbs state; do not be wise in your own eyes.

I took the ACT and SAT test so I could attend college. When I talked with Jonathan about going to school, earning a degree, and getting a job, he encouraged me but he never talked about what **_he_** was going to do. I kicked him to the curb as they say; we broke up, because of his lack of motivation. This really hurt him and he told me that I would be coming back to him.

After graduation I applied for and was accepted to the Cook County's Hospital Radiation Tech Program. I went to the interview and was given a tour of the facilities. Later, I received a letter informing me that I had to be eighteen years old to enter the program and that I had to wait for the next class session. I then enrolled into Malcolm X College and took Physics and Algebra. I was not aware of how much I did not learn in high school until I took those classes. I obtained a tutor and I passed both classes with Bs. My hard work paid off. Another ego boasts.

Mama instilled in me a strong work ethic and even though I lost a lot of that footing for a period of time, I came back to the very thing she taught me. I truly believe, if you pray hard enough, your children will return to those values, and they'll end up being really close to the people that you raised them to be. But, **you've** got to give it to your children, and you've got to give it to them **early**. Otherwise, the values will not manifest and take hold in the child's life.

Chapter 3

Pursuing My Dreams

I still love to sing, in spite of being beaten by my sister to harmonize. I auditioned for a singing group. This group was started by Robert, WVON's, a local radio station, disc-jockey. I was accepted after my second audition. We sang all the latest songs as Robert re-arranged them.

Discouragement from not starting the Radiation Tech Program caused me to enroll into a state funded training program where I obtained funds to attend the Omega School of Communications. I learned of this school from Robert's girl friend Pat. She attended there and obtained her Federal Communication Commission (FCC) license and worked as an engineer for WLS radio.

I earned my First class license and started applying to radio and Television stations in the area. I landed a job at CBS in the film library, logging old news shows from micro-film to prepare for computer transfer. While at CBS, I spoke to engineers and was told that I needed more training/education. I vowed that I would learn how to build my own Television or radio station. I even spoke to the lead anchor man at the time, Walter Jacobsen, who told me to get in front of the camera where the money is made. I should have taken his advice. Back then, when I got something in my head, it was hard to change my mind. Even now, I struggle with having tunnel vision.

One day, the Newsroom needed someone to answer the telephones. I volunteered. Every night during the News, I would answer the telephone in the Newsroom where the News was being filmed. My family and some friends saw me on TV. They would call the station to ask me questions about the News program. Another ego boasts. The job was temporary but I felt like hot stuff.

I was still in the singing group, performing at night clubs. Our group recorded a single, I've Got to Find a Way. It didn't sell very well. I started to date Robert and I would accompany him to the studio where he recorded commercials. I would work for free, I wanted the experience and he took advantage of that and our relationship. I knew that nothing would come of it. He was married and had a girlfriend. I think he rented the apartment for him and Pat because he had keys. He would take me to the apartment while his girlfriend was at work and we would have sex. It amazes me the risk I took.

There was no future with him. He did teach me a lot about communications and recording. I was deceived into thinking that I was having fun. Proverbs 14:12 states: there is a way that seems right to man but the end is death. (Emphasis added) Then one day a guy joined the singing group. He played keyboards. He is a fun loving guy. He liked to dance and danced very well. His name is Kevin.

One night the group went to a party at one of the member's house. I danced with Kevin and we did the bump, a popular dance at that time. Well, he had keys in his pocket and my hip was bruised. I don't remember it hurting. I was possibly too intoxicated to notice the pain. Robert stopped by the party and asked someone to see that I got home safely. After he left no one was interested in performing his request because I lived on the other side of town the north/west side, except Kevin. He got me home safely. Kevin was tall, dark, and chubby. He had a good sense of humor too. We would laugh and talk about everything. We were good friends. He started dating a girl name Shirley. She had other men that she saw but she captured Kevin before any of the other females got to him. Kevin and I still talked as friends.

The group had a concert in Indiana and Mama allowed me to go. Daddy was ill. He had brain cancer, so she was not herself. Robert arranged for me to have a room and I rode with Iris and her man friend John. Their room was connected to Robert's and mine. People were to think that Iris and I were sharing a room since John was married. But that was not the case. My best friend Rena was there with her boyfriend. She had tried to hook me up with him some months prior to this engagement. I did not like him for me. He was kind of nerdy and too light skinned. I liked men with more color than I had.

Kevin arrived at the hotel with Shirley. Later that evening everyone visited our room. We talked, drank, and got high. Shirley went to make a run and Kevin stayed behind. Iris went to John's room and the others left for their room. Kevin and I were alone. I kissed him and was not shy about making a pass. We hugged and kissed most of the night. I was not sure when Robert would return so we listened to the radio to determine when his show ended so he would not catch Kevin in the room. I don't know why I even cared about that, maybe because, he paid for the room. Shirley came to the room looking for Kevin, and he hid. She looked all over that hotel for him. The next day when Robert came to town, he heard about Shirley looking for Kevin. I told Robert that Kevin was in the room with me. He played it off until Kevin and I started spending more time together and I stopped having sex with him. Kevin and I could talk for hours. We went for walks, went to the movies, went shopping, all the things that a girl would love for her boyfriend to do with her. Anything I wanted he would buy. He was working as a teller for Hyde Park Bank and going to Loop College. He told me that he went to Shaw University in North Carolina for a while but dropped out and went on tour with a band. His father was sending him money for school and he was not paying tuition. He finally returned home after it was discovered that he was not attending school. He showed me pictures of him during that time and he was thin. He also told me about sexual exploits with his brother's white girl friend. I thought that was kind of low down of him and her. Now, look at the pot calling the kettle black. I was deceiving myself into thinking that since I did not know Robert's wife, I had no part in her pain. Kevin said that his brother did not know about his sexual encounter with his girlfriend. I doubt that.

Kevin and I started having sex. We would go to the Roberts Motel on King Drive. He knew how to set the mood. He changed the light bulbs to red ones and recorded a tape of my favorite music. He did all the right things but nothing happened that night. He could not get an erection. He even started crying because of it, my first moment of insight that I refused to accept. I tried to comfort him by saying that he was just nervous about our time together. On another occasion we went back to Roberts affectionately called "Bobs" and things worked better. I was feeling no pain, altered state/high, and he made a tape of Gino Vannelli's music, the music and the performer he liked. I was in heaven; at least it was heaven for what I knew at that time in my life. He performed oral sex and he was pretty good. I think I had one of my first oral organisms with him. I was hooked on oral sex. I asked, did he perform oral sex on Shirley and he said no. He told me that he

learned how to perform oral sex by reading a book. I sort of believed

him. He was a reader.

Chapter 4

Love in All the Wrong Places

Kevin and I were riding the bus, going to the south side of Chicago, on a hot summer's day and I started talking about moving in together. He agreed it would be nice. I introduced him to my daughter, Michelle (Shell). She liked him. Mama was leery of him until she heard him giggle. She told me, that she thought he was a man but realized that he was just a big kid. His size did fool people into thinking he was more mature than he actually was. Our talk went from living together to marriage.

During my courtship with Kevin my father was diagnosed with lung cancer which spread to his brain. He was very sick. He could not take care of himself. If he fell and we, my sisters and I tried to assist him, he did not want our help. He could not bare the thought that his female children were seeing him in this weakened state. My father said to me, "you are getting married; you should not be helping me". I told him, "daddy, if I can't help you, how can I help my future husband". He didn't have a response to that. We would prepare lunch for him and the kids, Shell, my nephew Dutch, and my niece Sandy. They would inform us if he wasn't eating. Shell, would say, "Granddaddy's not eating". It finally dawned on us that he wasn't swallowing. He forgot how because of the cancer in his brain. He then had to be admitted to a nursing home. Mama would visit him daily and tell us that he wanted to see us. She was also attending school to obtain her GED. I was so proud of her. Her determination was my motivation to never give up on anything I wanted in life. Little did I know that I would have to use this lesson in my life, caring for a sick husband and performing other responsibilities.

I could not bring myself to visit my father in that condition. I wanted to remember him as he was. Most of my sisters that visited, said that he did not know who they were. I did not want that memory.

I did not allow anyone to see me grieve for my father except Kevin. Sometimes the one person you share your deepest feelings with will use those feelings against you. Mama was upset with me for not showing any concern for my father. Her anger with me was not unusual, during our arguments she frequently referred to me as a whore and a slut. No wonder I had issues about sex. I would also stuff my feelings until they came out sideways.

I did not realize that my emotional needs were so intense that I frequently experienced depression. Little did she know I was just suppressing my feelings I had for my father's death. Later, I wished I had gotten to say goodbye to him. After my father's death, I could see how much he really loved me. He never showed it, with hugs and kisses, because he was not comfortable doing that, but his love was there just the same. If we asked, to kiss or hug him, he would not turn us away, but he did not initiate it. I discovered that even though a parent may love a child deeply, unless the child perceives that love he won't feel loved. This happens in other relationships besides parental relationships.

A little background on what lead to my father's illness: One day daddy was getting ready for work. He walked into the dining room and was overtaken with a seizure. The ambulance transported him to the hospital and that's when we discovered that he had lung cancer. He was administered radiation therapy, which burned his skin. I don't think chemotherapy was available then. The cancer was inoperable. It had spread to his brain. I later learned that when we lived on Gladys, years earlier, my dad was given a physical and was told that he had a spot on his lungs but did nothing about it. What a bummer. He may have still been alive if he had followed through.

Daddy always worked and played hard. He worked at a brass foundry. My father would come home from work, eat dinner, take a bath, and dress up to go out to gamble. Some mornings he would just come home in enough time to change into his work clothes and go to work. Little did I know that he had another place to sleep and a family. When he died we discovered his son by another woman.

We should have known that something was wrong with Daddy because he allowed my brothers to move in with us when their wives left them. They both had lost their jobs and were on drugs.

The day of daddy's funeral, I did not attend but stayed at the house for the re-pass. I had never attended a funeral and I was not going to start with my father. Mama thought I was being disrespectful; I was being a scared child, even though I was nineteen years old. Daddy died in July near his birthday, he was born on the 4th of July. Kevin and I were married on July 15th 1976. We didn't have much money, and we pulled together a reception in South Commons' party room. Mama told me to postpone the wedding. Mama did not want to attend the reception because I did not attend Daddy's funeral. I also passed out invitations to my reception at the re-pass; that was the icing on the cake for Mama. Her sister told her that I should get married because we all needed to move on with our lives.

After Daddy died and before I got married, I was rehearsing with my singing group and Shell was at home with Mama. Martha, one of my older sisters, was visiting, as she always did, on Saturday before her husband died. Dennis went into the bathroom and shot up drugs and left his works (drug paraphernalia) in the bathroom. Shell went in after him and came out with his needle. Martha lost it; she wanted to kill our brother. I missed all the excitement and Mama did not put him out. I dread to think what would have happened if Shell was harmed. That incident caused me to make a decision to move out sooner. My Mama and I had an argument and I told her that she was sending us a bad message, that it was ok to get high but not have sex. Shell and I went to Kevin's father's house where Kevin lived. Kevin checked us into a hotel. I don't know how Kevin paid for it. He probably got the funds from his dad. As stated earlier he was working at Hyde Park bank and the Playland at Foster Park. I can also speculate but I will not. We used all the money we had in a week and I asked Mama if I could return home. I wasn't working and Kevin could not afford the hotel or an apartment. Mama said yes, she thought I just wanted to be with Kevin and had no clue as to the real reason I left. Moving back home with Mama was not the answer, nothing had changed which led me to move sooner, and not using good judgment.

One weekend I wanted to go out but no one in the house would babysit Shell. I asked my sister Rhoda. She had Lana by this time, her youngest child. Lana was old enough to walk and talk. When I returned, I was told that Shell cut herself on the neck. The cut looked as if someone tried to pull a chain off her neck. Shell never told what happened and Rhoda did not know either. Apparently it happened while everyone was asleep. I could not figure out how this event took place and so I did not allow her to spend the night with my sister Rhoda for a long time.

Kevin was very different than other guys I dated. He was more attentive and loving. But there was also a mysterious side to him. His family kept secrets and he also developed that trait. They did not seem to acknowledge the things they knew others were doing wrong. For example, his aunt and uncle that lived with them were never married. This was not talked about and he only learned of this fact later in life. The reality of the situation was that the man was not his uncle but his aunt's live in lover. His life was also full of deception, just like mine. But I did not take the time to learn about this before marrying him.

We were married at city hall with Karl, Kevin's brother and Rhoda, my sister, as our witnesses. I stayed with Mama until we moved into our apartment on 99th and Perry. It was several month before we moved into our apartment. We visited "Bob's" a lot. For one of our honeymoon dinners, we went with friends to the Chicago Pizza and Oven Grinder. We also stayed in a hotel on the south side of Chicago. The next day we went to a carnival and returned to "Bob's" for a night of sex. I performed oral sex for him and licked every orifice. My performance started him to scream (like a woman) something I had never heard him do, my second moment of insight. Satan led me to believe that I was just that good to cause him to scream. We had sex regularly. It took time getting accustom to sleeping with a man all night.

We finally moved into the house on 9914 S Perry, in Chicago. My sister Martha and her family lived there prior to us. They recommended us to the landlord. While we lived there I was attending Chicago School of Automatic Transmission on the south side of Chicago. There were very few females in the school. Maybe ten and that's on the high end.

Kevin started going out with his friends. He would leave me at home alone. I would get upset with him. I would try to fight him but he would just hold my hands. He did not hit me. The house that we lived in was heated with gas and our gas bills were more then Kevin's check.

He would lie and say that he paid the bill. I would find out that he did not when the lights; phone or whatever was cut off. We borrowed, received money from his mother and father. His father would take us shopping for food. I did not know that Kevin's check could not cover our expenses. I trusted and believe that a husband was supposed to take care of his wife. That's what my dad did, even with his gambling habit. I thought he could provide for me and my child. He could not; my third moment of insight. I applied for public aid. Note I did not get a job. I also started going out with guys that would pay me for sex. That helped some. Kevin continued to go out with his friends. If he was not out with them he was on the telephone with them. We became like roommates just sleeping together and not having sex nor spending time together like we did before we were married.

Once Kevin and I married, emotionally, not much changed for me. This did not stop me from trying to find fulfillment through drugs or sex. I became involved easily, yet rejection frightened me. Married men were particularly attractive. I was married, they were married, I was not asking them to leave their wives, what could it harm? Do you see how wrong thinking can lead to wrong action? I was also attending school to become an auto-mechanic. I performed very well. I passed all test with Bs or better and learned to rebuild carburetors, change brakes, rebuild standard transmissions, etc. As long as I had power tools to loosen bolts, I could handle anything. But once I graduated, I could not find a job. No one wanted to hire an inexperienced female mechanic. One thing the interviewer would mention; that I would get dirty. I would then ask if they had soap and water. They would also tell me that I was too pretty to perform mechanic work. This was a classic case of sexual discrimination. You are probably wondering why auto-mechanics. Kevin told me that he had taken auto mechanics in school and I wanted to have something in common with him besides singing. He wasn't into cars it was just a class he took. He did enjoy building model cars.

    Kevin applied and was hired in Joliet by the State of IL. We moved to Joliet. Skeets, Kevin's step dad, gave us a Cadillac. It needed some work and Kevin and I worked on it prior to our move to Joliet. It needed ball joints and we installed them. I had never installed ball joints in school and did not know that a special tool was required to ensure that the ball is seated securely/locked in the joint.

One Saturday, we drove from Joliet to visit Kevin's mom in Chicago, on our way home, we pulled from the curd in front of her house and the wheel fell off. I was devastated. I remember saying thank God we were not on the highway. We spent the night with Kevin's mom and she paid for the car to be repaired.

We lived in the Chalet apartments in Joliet. We also bought a cocker spaniel and named him Buffy. After my father died, Mama moved to California. We sent Shell to live with her because we were having financial difficulties. Kevin would go to the store to steal food for us. It was very bad. I got so fed up with doing without and Kevin saying that he paid bills when he did not. I left him and went to live with Mama in California. We sold the dog to pay for the ticket. I did not realize that I would miss Kevin so much. He was at his mother's house most of the time at least that's what he said. I would call him everyday. I would charge the call to a phone number that was not mine. I wasn't the only one doing this at Mama's house either, which helped me to justify my behavior. Her two bedroom house was crowded. She had five people living there. While in California, I would walk Shell to and from school. I wanted to go back to Kevin in Joliet.

Nothing was happening for me in California. It was not like Soul Train, a teen program that was filmed and produced in California. Kevin purchased a ticket for me to return home and Shell was to return with Rhoda and her family. They had come to California for vacation. They planned to visit Disneyland. Shell wanted to go with them. She flew to Chicago with them when they returned. When I arrived in Illinois it was raining and Kevin was late picking me up from the airport. He had some excuse as to his tardiness but I did not believe him. We went home and had sex. His friend Carl had given him some pills that were suppose to help with stimulation and erections but it irritated me.

Kevin left the house for something and I went into Shell's bedroom and saw his attempt to clean up. He put all the garbage, clothes, plates, etc, into a big garbage bag and did not make the time to take the bag out. I started to empty the bag to get the clothes out and I found money in his shirt pocket. I never told him about it nor did he ask if I found anything. I did not know what I was returning to and reasoned that keeping the money was for my protection, more deceit.

I finally got a job working at Central High School (Central) as a teacher's aid/Para-professional. I worked with physically handicapped students. I learned a lot about tolerance working with those kids. I also learned that when you have a handicap you are not limited to your physical abilities. This was a great maturing experience for me.

If I stayed up late smoking marijuana, I would call in sick or say Shell was sick. Sometimes she would be, but I guess I had not matured enough and did not like going to work very much. I wanted a better paying job but I needed more training. At Central I met a teacher by the name of Thomas. He was married to a white woman name Jenny. He flirted with me everyday. His wife worked at the same school. I would come into his class with one of my students, to take notes for them, and he would make advances towards me. We finally connected sexually. While his wife was out of the house, we would have sex there. I was not using my head. When Kevin and Shell were not at home Thomas would come to our apartment to have sex. This would happen often and at various places. More examples of how wrong thinking leads to wrong action. Another sex partner I had during this time period was a bus driver name Joe, he was an older man. He sang with a gospel group. He would take me to a hotel to have sex. His penis could not keep an erection. I was fond of him. He had other girlfriends he had sex with too. He retired from the bus company when he developed diabetes. He informed me that he had a penis implant. I never had the opportunity to try it out.

I had a lot of men friends, a large number, and honey; I can't remember half of them. I wasn't intimate with all of them; it was just a matter of having somebody-anybody around because I felt my husband was not there for me.

Frankly, that's the dilemma so many women find themselves in. We've been so brainwashed into thinking that if we don't have a man, there's something wrong with us, like we're gay. That mind-set just begins a whole litany of bad decisions, and it invades other aspects of our lives. You find yourself making life choices based on a strategy of how to get another man.

Kevin, Shell, and I moved into another apartment in Joliet, on Richmond Circle. They were condos and we felt we were moving up. I was still working at Central High School. I applied for and was awarded a scholarship to attend Tuskegee Institute, in Alabama. The summer we moved into our new apartment I attended Tuskegee Institute's pre-engineering program. I took Math, Science, and English classes. I was also provided free room and board. Kevin and a friend of Jackie, Reynard, drove me there. Jackie stayed with Shell and our puppies.

Let me tell you about "the puppies". We were given a dog, a copper colored, Irish setter, name Pashum. She was house broken and good with Shell. We took her to the Vet and asked, "Could she be pregnant?" He said it was difficult for him to determine. Pashum would sleep in a box on the balcony. We noticed that she was scratching the box. We put a blanket in the box and thought it strange that she continued to scratch the box. My sister and her kids came to visit and when the kids went on the balcony, Pashum started to bark. We did not understand her behavior. One morning I decided to stay home from work. I was lying in bed as it rained. Pashum was in her box, as the rain became heavier, I went to the door to pull her box inside the apartment and saw her delivering puppies. I freaked. I did not know what to do. I continue to pull the box into our bedroom and then called a Vet and asked, "What should I do". I was told, "nothing, she knows what she's doing". Pashum delivered five puppies. We went from having one dog to six. We had to wait until they were weaned before we could give them away. We waited at least four weeks. This was a miracle that God allowed me to experience. Wow, what a blessing, it was funny having those little puppies running around that apartment. They slept in our bedroom and we would help her feed them. They would wake up crying and we would position them on her nipples. Then their eyes opened and they started to move around more. It was as if we had babies, well, they were our babies. Pashum would allow Kevin and me to pick them up and clean them off. One day Shell picked up one of the puppies and Pashum snapped at her. I told Pashum, "You would not like it if I hurt your baby so don't hurt mine." Pashum held her head down in submission to my authority but I told Shell not to touch the puppies without us being present. We named them all too. We kept one of the puppies, Shell named him Billy.

When I returned from Tuskegee, We gave the dogs away. I enrolled into DeVry Institute of Technology and would not have the time to care for the dogs.

Chapter 5

Drugs

I was turned on to freebasing. I would get high with my little sister Jackie and one of her guy friends.

Later during her drug-addiction she declared that she was gay. My brother-in-law, Chicken introduced Jackie to this demonic substance. I remember her not being able to speak after taking a hit of cocaine. It was like her month was frozen and she could not say the words she wanted to speak. She felt kind of embarrassed by this and I felt sad for her and felt that she was out of control. Her use was more frequent than mine and at this time and she was addicted. I could not understand how a person could get hooked on this substance. I distinctly remember wondering what it would be like being hooked. Beware of what you wonder about, because you will surely get it. While attending college I would go to Chicago on weekends to get high. I trivialized my actions. I told myself that I was not addicted and was just partying on the weekend.

The drug addictive spirit and homosexuality spirit always attach themselves to victims of either one or all of these things, molestation, rape, verbal and/or physical abuse and a lack of demonstrated love. The person may have also been subjected to watching someone else fall victim to these things. It is sometimes a generational curse. The homosexual spirit and the drug addictive spirit entwines themselves so deeply within, no one can tell you that it is not you (1). I also claimed that I was bi-sexual because of my relationship with Lara, a young lesbian I met at school. Another excuse I used was; I needed a break and reward for working hard at school. I would get high with my brother-in-law Chicken, the one I would chase off the couch as a kid, and his friends. Occasionally my sister Rhoda would join us but she was having trouble breathing after taking a hit and had to stop getting high or she would have died. But her husband did not stop using and only death stopped him. Chicken introduced the whole family that was interested in getting involved, to freebasing. We were deceived into thinking that we were having fun. Just like with the other drugs, I used,

I thought I was having fun. Always inside there was a void that relationships, drugs, and alcohol could not fill.

Kevin and I moved from Richmond Circle to Buell St. I also had many lovers visit this house while Kevin was at work and Shell was either at school, work or in Chicago. I would occasionally spend the weekend with my gay cousin Karla and visit gay bars to flirt with woman. While at my cousin's house I would snort cocaine. I met a black female lawyer by the name of Carmine. She was married and had a child. I felt she was experimenting sexually. Kevin and I visited her house to try to build a friendship but Carmine said she was not interested in sleeping with Kevin. I was not looking for sexual partners but I guess she thought that was why we came to visit. Her husband was a graphics artist for channel 5 News. I started dating another married woman named Barb, who's white; we would have sex when she visited our apartment. On several occasions I even spent the night at her house while her husband was out of town. I met her at a gay bar in Joliet. She was unable to have children. She and her husband planned to adopt the foster children they had. They fostered a Hispanic girl and an African American baby boy. There was an investigation and talk that her husband may have raped the little girl. She told me that her husband made accusations about catching her and Suzy, the Hispanic foster child, in bed together. Knowing Barb, I don't doubt it. She divorced her husband and became very attached to me. I was not leaving Kevin, at that time, so we had to cool out. Barb found a guy who wanted to marry her and she planned to return the foster children because he did not want children especially minorities. I was so upset with her. I told her that she should not have taken those children if she didn't plan to keep them until they were grown. I also told her that she was selfish and was only thinking of herself. Now, look at me judging her. She told me that she wanted a fresh start. I never spoke to her again, as you can probably tell. Some people's lives are filled with daily abuse, it is all they know; it becomes a way of life. Satan knows and is just waiting for the door of opportunity to come in.

Let's re-visit, Tuskegee, Alabama. The summers were scorching hot. I would awaken to temperatures over 80 degrees. I did not enjoy being there. I was not accustomed to being away from home for an extended period of time. I was out of my comfort zone. I missed Kevin and Shell. I endured an uncomfortable bus ride to return home. My dorm mates gave me a going away party. When I returned home I enrolled into DeVry Institute of Technology with the help of my best friend Rena. She gave me the registration fee. I did very well there too but I wanted to go further than the associate degree they offered, so I transferred to Joliet Junior College, (JJC). My GPA for the quarter at DeVry was also over 3.5. All credits from DeVry did not transfer to other colleges. The electronic courses I took there had to be re-taken. While at JJC, I enrolled in Math and Science courses in preparation to go on to obtain a Bachelors degree in Engineering. I graduated from JJC with three Associates degrees. My GPA there was over 2.5 but not 3.0. A guy that Kevin rode to work with also drove me to school. As a matter of fact, his name was Kevin too. I had to ride the bus home from school.

My first summer at JJC, I met Lara Tanner, a deaf gay woman with a three year old daughter. Lara was living with her parents when we met. We were in the same trigonometry class. I met her parents when we studied at their home. As you can tell we hit it off. I started spending a lot of time with her. I don't quite remember how we got on the subject of her being gay but I was interested. I told her of my encounter with females as a child, and that was an open door for that demonic spirit. *God is a spirit. Angels are spirit beings. The devil is a spirit being and so are his demons. Spirits need a body in which to reside. One or two spirits governs us. God or the devil. God uses people to do his will and so does the devil. This is why we wrestle not against flesh and blood (2).* Lara was also a recovering heroine addict. She developed migraine headaches and, for relief, would take codeine. She would also go to the emergency room to get a shot of Demerol. She did this so often the hospital stopped administering her shots. She was also prescribed codeine. The doctors stopped writing her prescriptions. Then she started writing her own, until the pharmacy caught on. She told me that her mom was addicted to pills when she was younger and she was continuing that tradition. The migraine headaches were her justification. When the source of codeine and shots from the emergency room dried up, she enrolled in a methadone program. She said she needed something to stop the headaches. Oh, I forgot to tell you, she's white. My spirit did not feel good about her drug use. But I did not stop associating with her. We smoked weed, marijuana. I was deceived into thinking that marijuana was ok compared to other drugs. During the 1970s, 80s, and 90s, society did not think a person was a drug addict if they smoked marijuana. Many people had either smoked it or were smoking it. As you see, I got accustom to smoking it. *The drug-addicted personality has those same deep-rooted hurts and pains as previously mentioned. These pains often go hidden for many years like a hidden disease slowly growing and poisoning the system. Anytime we need any kind of outside stimulant in order for us to feel good or to have fun, this is a sign of something being wrong. The enemy is deceptive, sneaky, and very subtle. You continue to use because you think you like it. By the time you realize you have a problem you are already addicted and that stronghold demon is already in the house. Like any prescribed drug, the longer you use it the more the dosage must be increased in order for it to work. The thing that helped you in the beginning has now turned on you and become your enemy (3).*

    Kevin had no problem with my relationship with Lara. He even seemed to be kind of happy about it. I felt I loved her. Then she and Kevin became kind of close and I suspected that they were having an affair. I knew she would have sex with men, because she had a child. Looking back, those two spirits were just working against me. Lara moved from her parent's house and moved in with a male friend. I came out to family and friends as bi-sexual. This admission really affected my daughter and she started misbehaving.

    After her male friend moved out, Lara gave me a key to her apartment. Michelle was also given a key. She would go there after school and I would pick her up after work. Shell's school was located next door to Lara's apartment. One day, Shell bought a few of her friends to Lara's apartment and some of Lara's money was stolen. Shell said that she did not take it and I was not sure. I made her pay back the money. I took her to a lawyer to scare her into thinking that Lara was going to press charges and she would be thrown into jail. The lawyer played alone and she was very scared. Kevin's dad then started giving her an allowance and said it would stop her from stealing. We felt we could not afford to give Shell an allowance. She was provided with the necessities. Some children did not even get that. Giving Shell the allowance was a good idea. After this incident, I tried to explain to her that because I was bi-sexual did not mean that she would be.

I graduate from JJC while we lived on Buell St in Joliet. My family attended the graduation. I wanted to celebrate, by myself, of course to get high. I went to my Friday night spot in Sell's basement on the west side of Chicago. I enjoyed getting high. My sister Rhoda showed up there too, to both of our surprise. Kevin seemed disappointed but did not put up a fight about me having my own way. He never did, that made me feel that he did not care. I would say he was being a martyr when he sacrificed for me. I later learned that he was showing love for me.

Sell became a sex partner and he confided in me that Chicken told him to take me for all my money. I told him, "I don't have any money and I just graduated and do not have a job yet". He told me to watch out for Chicken. He said that Chicken was using me. Well, I sort of knew that but I reasoned that it was part of the territory of drug use. Most of our deception comes from deception of self. This is the most dangerous. It will lead you straight to hell.

Shell would go to Chicago every weekend to spend the night at Natalie's or Mama's house. I taught her to ride the bus to Chicago. She became proficient enough to ride the bus alone. After a while, Natalie told me that Shell should not come to visit so often. I was hurt by this. She only visited on the weekend but I guess she wanted a break too.

I was being inconsiderate of her as she was to me when our kids were toddlers and I would bathe Shell and Sandy. The kids liked taking a bath together.

I felt that Natalie had her three kids, what trouble would one more be? That was inconsiderate of me and her calling me out on it, hurt. Mama allowed Shell to sleep in her apartment and go upstairs to play with Natalie's kids.

During those weekends Shell was away, Kevin and I were involved in various activities that involved getting high. One such incident was our third year wedding anniversary where I invited some friends over for an orgy. Most men would have jumped at this but Kevin was concerned about what to do if he could not perform. I told him to perform oral sex. It started with me inviting my best friend Rena. When I invited her, Bobby and John were visiting her house and they wanted to participate. Bobby bought his girlfriend KC. It was not what I expected and I was un-happy that I let it become what it became. After the event, it was interpreted as a non sexual event, a lying on of hands. But people did pair up to have sex, Kevin and KC, Rena and Bobby, and John and I. They all thought I was enjoying myself with John because of the sounds I made, as I said, I was into denial about a lot of things and enjoying sex with some men was one of them. I would fake, to allow men to think they were really turning me on, most where not. When I accepted Jesus as my Lord and Savior and discovered what love is, I stopped faking. If the sex did not feel good I would tell my husband.

I connected sex with love. As I think about it, I had better sex with people I did not love. I thought about myself and not them. But once I allowed God to come into my life, sex was different. I'm getting ahead of myself, back to life with Kevin. After the orgy event I talked to KC about getting together again, she said yes but nothing happened. I was too insecure to let it happen again. I thought my husband liked her better than he liked me. I wasn't going to chance it. We told people about the orgy and the guys thought it was cool. Most of the woman just looked at us as those freaky Wilson's. We also had a pajama party while living in that same apartment. We invited our neighbors so they would not complain about the noise. None came. The night of the party there was a blizzard, so people stayed overnight. We catered food from Lee and Eddies and people bought alcohol and drugs. We also provided drugs, marijuana and acid.

I remember that it was the first time that Donald, my nephew, had taken acid. He had just gotten discharged from the military. He freaked out from the acid. We finally got him to calm down. Even while taking drugs, if others family members were freaking out or not doing well with the experience, I would talk them down. It's as if I was no longer high, and I led them out of their bad experience. That was another reason I deceived myself into thinking I had things under control. *There are functional alcoholics and drug dependent personalities. They keep their jobs and function daily. These people are less likely to realize that they are sick inside and need deliverance (4).* This was me. Now back to the pajama party, many of the guys thought that we were going to engage in an orgy. But that did not happen. I had enough of orgies for a while.

I would ask Rena, my best friend, to visit our place or Kevin and I would go to hers to have sex as a group. Since her divorce I tried to make her a part of our life. She's an only child and I felt that she needed re-assuring that someone loved her besides her mom and aunt. There I go again, trying to take care of somebody. I felt that no one took care of me. What I put out, I was not getting back but my motive for putting out was for people to like me. I was a big time people pleaser. I was disappointed often because others did not reciprocate which led to more escapism.

Rena turned me on to opium. She went to Detroit and returned with a large quantity of opium from her cousin. We would roll it like a child would make a snake or worm with play dough. We would put these opium worms into marijuana joints. Of course, Kevin bought an opium pipe. We had quite a bit of drug paraphernalia. Opium is like heroine. Since I was not shooting it into my veins, I would justify the use of it.

Boy did we get high a lot. As I said early, I started with marijuana and I progressed to smoking opium. One thing I told myself was that I would never shoot drugs into my veins. My brothers turned me off on that. I hated them for doing it and living in mama's house. *There always has to be an open door for these types of spirits mentioned earlier to come in. From having endured or having watched some of the previously mentioned abuses, feelings such as hurt, pain, anger, unforgiveness, and bitterness have set in. Which can be the keys to opening the door to those stronghold spirits (5).*

Let me tell you a story about rationalization. A Mr. Jones rationalized not paying his parking tickets and went to prison for failure to pay. When asked why he didn't just pay the tickets? He answered, 'They were just parking tickets; it was no big deal.' Then one day the police arrived at his home at 4:00am, put him in a big black bus, and took him to court. As he stood before the judge, he said, 'Your honor, I bought seven hundred dollars with me to pay the tickets and to cover the court cost.' The judge said, 'Mr. Jones, I'm going to save you all that money. You are going to jail!' Mr. Jones was terrified.

His big mistake was that he trivialized his crimes by thinking that they were "just" parking tickets, and so he deceived himself, like I did about getting high. Had he known the judge's ruling (that he would go to prison), he would have immediately made things right between himself and the law.

Most of us realize that we have broken God's law—the Ten Commandments, but it's no big deal. Let me ask you a few questions about the laws you have broken and see if it's a big deal. Have you ever lied? You say, "Yes. But they were only white lies. They were nothing serious." Have you ever stolen something? You say, "Yes, but only little things." Can you see what you are doing? You are trivializing your crimes, and like Mr. Jones, you will deceive yourself. What you are doing is saying that you haven't actually "sinned," and the Bible warns, "He who says he has no sin deceives himself." The truth is; if you have lied, then you are a liar. If you have stolen anything (the value of the item stolen is irrelevant), you are a thief.

What you and I need to hear is the judge's ruling for lying and stealing. Here it is: "All liars shall have their part in the lake which burns with fire and brimstone" (Rev.21:8).

All unrepentant liars go to hell. You say, "I don't believe in hell." That's like someone saying to the judge, "I don't believe in jail." What we believe or don't believe does not change realities. No unrepentant thief will enter heaven. Not one.

Thank God for Jesus and his love for us that rightful judgment I should receive has been eliminated when I accepted Jesus as my Lord and Savior. Of course I have to continue to walk in his ways, but I grieve about where I could be going if I had not changed my ways. The

Bible says, "For by grace you have been saved through faith, and that not of yourselves; it is the gift of God, not of works, least anyone boast" (Eph2: 8-9) Now, let's go back into how deceived I became before coming to this revelation.

While living on Buell, I enrolled in Illinois Institute of Technology (IIT) for the fall term. The credits from JJC transferred and I was in my third year for some courses but had to take freshman electronics courses and classes that JJC did not offer that was required for graduation. My daily routine was to ride a six am bus to downtown Joliet then ride a bus going to Chicago. My classes started at nine but I had to leave early because of the bus schedule. I would get out of school at three or four depending on what day of the week it was. I would return to Joliet after six pm. I kept this schedule for two years. I would come home some days and want to quit. Kevin would encourage me to go back. He was very supportive of me going to school.

At the beginning of our marriage Kevin and I started out sleeping together then I wanted to sleep in another room because his snoring was interrupting my sleep. We tried a few remedies but none seem to help him.

One Christmas break he sent me on a five day trip to the Bahamas. His friends and colleagues told him that he was crazy. He told them, "Mary doesn't have to go out of town to sleep with anyone; She could do that at home". He was right on that. Kevin even recorded a cassette tape of music for me. I bought some cocaine from Chicken to take on the trip. I carried it in the lining of a sanitary napkin. I was not on my period and we did not have the airport security that we currently have. Little did I know, I would hook up with Julian, a native, that had better quality cocaine than I and he also freebased. I went on one excursion with the tour group; the rest of the time was spent with Julian, getting high. While at Julian's apartment, I played the tape Kevin made which sounded like a make out tape. I was not interested in making out, only getting high. But all men who get high want to have sex. I allowed him to perform oral sex. Before having oral sex, Julian had eaten a tuna salad sandwich, with black pepper. My genitals were on fire from the pepper and I had to run cold water on them. My hotel room had a refrigerator and stove. I went shopping and bought food to cook but most of the time I was at Julian's. I got high so much that it scared me and I wanted to go home. I could not arrange that. I had to stick it out.

Upon arrival to Chicago's O'Hare Airport, I waited for Kevin to pick me up. I was cold and coming down from a five day high. I was not a happy camper. I did not take my coat to the Bahamas, and Kevin was to bring it from home. As I said earlier, I went during Christmas break. I shared with Lara how I felt addicted to the drug. But I did not pursue getting more until the weekend and during school breaks. The drugs in the states did not compare to the drugs I had in the Bahamas. Of course I thought I had it under control because the drugs were cut, not as potent, but they could hook you just the same. The things they cut it with, to increase the quantity, could cause hallucination or even death.

I graduated from IIT and was hired as an Electrical Engineer by Rockwell International. I made electrical drawings for the printing presses they built using CADCAM. Financially things changed for Kevin and me. We had more money to do more things like get high. I bought a New Jeep Wrangler. My license plates read, NOTHIS 8.

Everyone would ask what NOTHIS meant, and I would tell them that it meant that the car was mine and not Kevin's. I was paying for it. Drug testing for jobs was not required. There was a guy at Rockwell who was interested in me. We talked daily. I finally consented to see him while I was at a hotel for the States of IL's Christmas party. Kevin was DeeJaying for the party. I planned to get high but I also met the guy from work there and of course we had sex. After he left I went to the Christmas party, left early and called my friend Perry to get high. We were still getting high when Kevin entered the room. He wanted to sleep so Perry left. Nothing was said about Perry being in the room, except when did I call him.

I worked for Rockwell for about six or eight months. Ronald Regan was President and enforced many cut backs and companies laid people off. Last hired, first fired, as they say. I was one of the casualties. I filed for unemployment and started looking for employment in my field. I didn't get a nibble. I applied for a teaching position to teach electronics at ITT Technology Institute. I was interviewed and subject matter tested and offered a job. They also did not perform a drug test. This was the winter of 1991. Thank God I had a Jeep. I had to drive from Joliet to Hoffman Estates daily. I performed very well there. I was not using cocaine regularly during this time period, although I would occasionally smoke weed.

My oldest brother Bug, the gay one, the familiar spirit, moved back home with Mama. He had been using drugs and acted as if he had lost some of his mental abilities. He loved playing the lottery. I don't know how the nickname Bug came about, as stated earlier he was named for my father, Roland. Bug enrolled in a nursing school and was performing well. I even helped/tutored him with his studies, Math and Chemistry. One Saturday, Kevin and I went to visit Mama, we had some potent weed. Kevin went into the basement to get high with Dennis and Bug. When they came upstairs Bug passed out in the hallway. As we were trying to revive him, he came to and thought he fainted because he won the lottery. Mama was upset with Kevin for getting him high; but Bug was a grown man and older than Kevin. Bug, graduated from nursing school and was working at a local hospital as a

RN (Registered Nurse). His goal was to obtain a Bachelor's degree in nursing and become a Physician's Assistant.

One day after work, he went to Chicken's apartment to buy drugs, of course he would be using some of the drugs with Chicken. He told my sister that he was going out for one last fling before starting school. Little did he know it was going to be a literal last fling. We never know the day or the hour we will be called home from the earth. Bug left Chicken's place and went to a hotel with one of the boys from the neighborhood. Mama was called late at night with the news that he was found dead in a hotel. Dennis went to the hotel and found him sitting in a chair. We later learned that he had a seizer and the boy left him in the hotel room. This incident stopped our drug use for a little while.

ITT Technical Institute was planning to build a new school in Matteson and I wanted to transfer there. We moved into a house on Western Ave. While living there, I had a hysterectomy and Shell had a mastectomy. She was twenty-one years old. This really affected her. I prayed that God would spare her and take me. He was not ready for me or her. I also prayed that she would not loose her hair during chemo therapy. God's faithful and he answered my prayers. Kevin was very supportive during this time. After my operation, the doctor said that I should be kept awake because I would stop breathing because of the anesthesia. Kevin sat by my bedside and kept me awake. My sister Marsha was also there but she could not tolerate seeing me that way. She said I looked like I was dying. I would have died if I was not awaken and reminded to breathe.

Chapter 6

The Betrayals

More information on Shell's breast cancer: One Saturday, we went to Mama's house and Shell told her about a lump she had under her arm. Mama encouraged her to have it checked out. I went to the clinic with her and the doctor performed a needle biopsy. The results were positive for cancer and they wanted to perform a mastectomy. She was only twenty-one years old. We both cried. Remember I prayed to God that he would not take her life, and I asked him to take mine instead? Thank God that he had something else for me to do. Shell's self-esteem plummeted. She thought that no man would want her without a breast. She was also told that she should not have children because of the chemo therapy. Shell met a smooth talking young man that had been in prison. Without our knowledge, she married this abusive man some time around New Years. She was still living with us after she married him. One weekend he came to visit and they told us of their marriage. I was very upset with her. I did not want to speak to her. While I was not speaking to her Kevin stayed in contact. He would come home from work and tell me of his conversations with her. I felt betrayed and hurt and did not want to hear anything about her. Shell's husband would fight her and forced her to stay away from her family. Every time she would call the police and put him out, she would let him back in. We allowed her to stay with us but she would return to him. One Saturday she brought her husband to Mama's house. Shell and I had a big argument; little did I know that I caused some of her beatings by being against her husband. Mama told her that the boy was not welcome in her house. Of course this enraged Shell. I was then called every name except a child of God. Mama was not having it and told them to leave.

The straw that broke the camels back for Shell was her husband breaking her nose. She then wanted to come back home. I told her that she could return home if she had counseling for self-esteem. She went to the Guardian Angel home to receive counseling. I then allowed her to move in.

I started working at the Matteson campus of ITT after healing from my hysterectomy. Kevin and I were still not sleeping in the same bedroom. Our relationship seemed to get better at least for me when Shell was out of the house. After she moved back in, Kevin's dad became very ill; he went into the hospital and died. I remember becoming very ill at work and my boss drove me home while another staff member drove my car. When I arrived home, I discovered that Kevin's dad had died around the time I became ill.

Kevin's dad left an inheritance for his children and grandchildren. He left Kevin and me over $20,000. We were able to pay off all our bills and put a nice down payment on a $200,000 home. Shell and I went hunting for homes. We saw many models and chose a few for Kevin to review. We decide on a four bedroom house with a loft and cathedral ceiling in the den/family room. It also had a living room, dining room and kitchen with marble counter tops. We borrowed some of the designs from the models and incorporated them into our home. I decorated the entire house, chose colors for the inside, and Kevin chose the color for the outside. He coordinated with the inside. The theme of the house was cream, black, grey, and white. To be different, Kevin painted his room a dark blue with green molding. We took pictures of the whole process, from staking the land to digging the hole, pouring concrete to putting on the roof. We kept a photo album to remember it all. I chose the master bedroom with the attached bath with a whirl pool. There was also a separate shower in this bathroom. We installed gold doors on the shower stall. The fixtures were brass. The wall and counter tops were white. The color theme was white and gold/brass. The bathroom was huge. I put an étagère, chair, and hamper in this bathroom. I had a phone installed. It was my special place.

I paid attention to every detail when decorating the house. From the rugs, curtains, art work, candles, knickknacks, and paint. This was a showplace. We invited our family to view it and they loved it. I also bought a puppy, a miniature salt and pepper schnauzer, I name him Petey. He was very lovable. All looked good on the outside. Everybody thought that we had big money and had it "going on". But there was no happiness in the house. I was getting high almost every weekend and Kevin was performing gigs with his friend Mike. He would return from work and remove his clothes and leave them in the kitchen area. I constantly picked up after him. I started paying for a house cleaning service. They cleaned the entire house except Kevin's room. Kevin's room was like a war zone. In his room, he had equipment, clothes, paper, dirty dishes, and food. When we had sex he would come to my bedroom. There was no romance; I would get with him to have an oral orgasm. He was very good at oral sex. We started going to counseling again. It did not resolve anything; it produced the same results the previous years counseling session produced. I was getting high a lot too. At this time, I didn't want to be set free; I didn't know I was in captivity.

My family thought Kevin and I had a lot of money. We were both working, but we had no liquid cash on hand for emergencies. We had credit cards and a line of credit from a second mortgage. But we did not have money as people assumed.

Chicken goes to purchase a large quantity of crack for me. I waited at his apartment for hours; I realized that he cut the merchandise so he could return with a large portion of the product for himself, as he always did. I informed him that I was purchasing the drugs for someone else. But that did not stop his usual behavior.

When I would buy drugs from Chicken, he would charge me double and give me less. His son would do the same. My younger sister Jackie and my older brother Dennis who were also hooked on drugs started living with Chicken. Dennis' old girlfriend, Tiny was dating Chicken. Dennis moved out. Jackie stayed with Chicken and Tiny for a short time after Dennis moved. Jackie moved after she went off on them for using her. Chicken would use his own mother. He is pure evil. Not mean, charismatic, in fact, but actually caring for someone seemed totally out of character for him. If you remember I recognized this in him when I was just a toddler. I pray for him but I think he has chosen his side. He speaks of Allah and not God. *We are spirit beings that are fighting a spiritual adversary. We cannot win any battle until we identify the enemy (6)*

I wanted Mama to move into our house but she refused. We told her that we would build a room on the main level so she would not have to climb the stairs. But she did not feel comfortable with that arrangement. Mama had emphysema. She was very ill. Her breathing capacity was diminishing everyday. I felt she was holding on for my younger sister

Marsha, who would not let her go. Mama and I talked about her dying and I asked if she could, would she come back to talk to me. Of course she said yes. Now I know better than to want to speak to the dead but at that time I just wanted some hope of making contact with her again. Since I accepted Jesus as my Lord and Savior, I will see her again.

Mama died just before Thanksgiving. Kevin was at the hospital visiting her the morning before she died and asked that I come to visit. He felt that she was not going to make it through the night. On her previous stays in the hospital, I would call her instead of visiting. This was the only time I visited her in that hospital. I did not like hospitals and I got physically ill when I visited them. But I came that day. I learned that she was blind and had lost her vision months earlier. The strong concentration of oxygen she had to use caused the blindness. I was not aware that pure oxygen could cause blindness. Mama was in a semi-conscious state when I entered her room. Her oxygen was set to the max. She looked as if she was talking to someone that we could not see. She was shaking her head no. I asked was she in pain and she shook her head no. I surmised that she was telling who ever was there not to take her, yet. I went to Natalie's apartment and told her that we needed to inform the other siblings of Mama's condition. The doctor called prior to my arrival to inform her.

    I drove back, to Joliet, and stayed in the house. I received a call from Natalie stating that the hospital had called and stated that Mama was near death and if we wanted to see her one last time, we had better get there fast. Natalie and Marsha headed to the hospital. I headed back to Chicago. They told me of the opposition they met trying to see Mama before she died. One, being traffic, when there is usually none during the late night/early morning hours. Another, the parking garage at the hospital would not allow them to enter. Once they gained access; they had to get to the floor where her room was located. Another obstacle was; the floor was blocked because it was after visiting hours. They had to convince the guard that the hospital had called them. Upon arrival to Mama's room, she had passed. Natalie said Mama's skin was still warm. Mama told us that she never wanted any of us to be present when she died; this is one reason why she did not want us to stay at the hospital.

At first I was only getting high on the weekend. Then I started getting high daily. I even got high before going to work. Shell had moved into her own apartment by this time. Kevin and I turned her bedroom into a huge walk in closet. We installed shelves and closet hangers for our clothes. We also kept the iron and ironing board in the room and the room became our dressing room. Kevin was still doing his thing and I was doing mine. Then Kevin quit his job and enrolled in school without informing me. For extra money I started teaching an evening Math class at the Community College. Kevin would return home hours after school was out. We would argue about this but it did not change.

I became more frustrated and started looking for an apartment. I found one a few miles from work in Richton Park, the same building my secretary lived in. While Kevin and I were living together he would occasionally comment about me getting high but he never said directly to me, "I think you are getting out of control and should get some help". I felt that if we were not going to act like husband and wife, I should be living someplace else. He said that he did not want me to leave but could not stop me. There was a blizzard the weekend I was supposed to move and the truck drivers cancelled. I moved the following weekend. I told Kevin, that I needed some space and time to work things out.

I also told him that if I decided to return and he had someone else, I would not get upset because I left. He said that he did not plan to hook up with anyone. But as soon as I left he was gone more than at the house. He was hanging out with his "school friends".

I liked the apartment in Richton Park. My cousin Anna also lived in the same building. We only spoke in passing. Everything seemed to be fine. But I was still getting high on the weekends in Chicago. Then I started getting high in my apartment. One night I was taking a hit in the bathroom and I walked out to go to the bedroom and someone said hi. The sound came from the linen closet, that freaked me out but I did not say a word. The apartment was dark, so they could have been in the apartment, but I don't remember hearing anyone leave, so I'm not sure if I was hearing someone from another apartment. Then everything started to go a little crazy. I would think that people had come into the apartment while I was out. One morning on the way to work I saw a guy looking into an apartment from the patio wall. It looked like my apartment but I was running late so I did not investigate. Sometimes I would come home for lunch to get high. I would return to work but I knew I was out of control. I started seeing Robert again. My life was becoming uncontrollable. One weekend I invited a couple of people to my apartment to get high. Then Kevin and his friends started to go to Chicken's house. They would do things to freak me out. For example, if I laid an item down it would be moved to another location. I would ignore these antics but I was still freaked. I told Chicken I knew what was happening and wished that people would just leave me alone and move on with their life. Then Chicken said, "I did not think you knew what was going on". He said, "You were so cool about it." Well of course I wanted to be cool. But it did not stop the fact that they were trying to play mind games with me. I no longer felt safe in my apartment and asked Kevin could I move back into the house.

I returned to the house we built the spring of 1999; big mistake. I stayed in the house getting high, freaking out about every noise I heard. Kevin and his friends would come in and do things to freak me out there too. Let me take a diversion to tell you how I received confirmation. I had been away from the house a few months and moved into a new apartment with my new boyfriend Ron. The house had gone into foreclosure and was on the market. A friend of my friend, Barbara, not the white woman, went to view the house. He told her about this nice house he considered. He also told her what the next door neighbor told him about the man, who formerly lived in the house. He said the man was trying to run his wife crazy. Barb's friend does not know me or Kevin. He had no idea that what he was telling Barb was going to help someone that she knew. Do you see how God orchestrates things to give one confirmation? I was beginning to think that it was only my imagination because of the drugs. Oh, how deceived I was.

Now back to the house, one weekend I was getting high and wanted some attention from Kevin. I told him that I was going to kill myself. He called Lara who spoke to me. Then Kevin went to pick up Lara and left me at home alone. Now let's get real, if he was concerned about me killing myself, why would he leave me alone and drive over fifty miles to get someone to talk to me? At least Lara called the police who came to the house to speak to me. I told them that my husband and I were having troubles and I was depressed and just wanted some attention, so they left. But Kevin left me before the police arrived. Lara spent the night and talked me into getting help. My understanding was that I could sign myself out of the facility. That was not the case. I was first admitted to a ward with mentally challenged people. I stayed in bed most of the time because of the drugs they administered. I was upset that I was not receiving help. I told Kevin, I could medicate myself. He spoke to someone and I was moved to the ward for substance abusers. I learned to tell people what they wanted to hear, another act of deception. I was so upset that I threatened Kevin to have me released. He did not want me home. I talked to Shell and she said that she would sign me out. She came and took me home. Once home I went out to get high. I was going to show them, I thought. This was my stay in the funny farm. I was prescribed anti-psychotic medication, and anti-depressants, more drugs. On March 28, 2000, I was in my room getting high; I received a phone call informing me that my brother Norris had died. As I walked toward the stairs I could hear the sound of oral sex. I ran down the stairs as Kevin's friend was quickly leaving. I started hitting and screaming at Kevin. He finally left the house. And I went back to getting high. He later called to ask if I was ok. I was so angry with him, I don't remember what I said but it was probably not nice. He did not come home that night. But he went to the court house the next day and filed an order of protection against me. I probably told him that I would kill him. Then I filed one on him. Kevin did not return home. He stayed in a hotel with his friend. He told my sister Natalie and my daughter, and even his mother that I tried to kill him. He also told them that the drugs were causing me to hallucinate and that I thought I saw him with someone.

The final event after returning to the house Kevin and I built. One afternoon, I went to the store to buy food. I returned home and microwaved a macaroni and cheese meal. I went upstairs to use the bathroom. As I was sitting on the toilet, several policemen came into the house to remove me. When I entered the house I had locked the door. Kevin accompanied them and used his key to gain access. I told the officers I was not leaving. I would not get off the toilet. I started crying and asked them how they would feel if someone came into their house while they were on the toilet and asked them to leave. The officers felt sorry for me and called an ambulance that drove me to the hospital because Kevin told them that I was suicidal. I guess my behavior didn't waver from that description. I had written a note stating that I wanted to die and left it on the stairs days before this incident. It was not there when I returned from shopping. Kevin had that note and he gave it to the policemen. Remember he was staying in a hotel. How did he get the note? Our dog did not give it to him. I was there with the dog by myself and he was supposed to be afraid for his life. This is just more proof that he would come into the house without my knowledge. He would say that I was hallucinating and that I imagined him there.

Chapter 7

Meeting God near The Edge

Once at the hospital I talked with my drug counselor and told her that I had no place to stay. Upon release, I got into my car and a police officer returned to the house with me to retrieve some clothes. I remember sleeping in the car, in the garage, until Kevin returned home. Kevin paid for a hotel that night because he did not want me in the house. That worked for one night. I still needed a place to stay.

Kevin's sister, Liza, allowed me to stay at her place with his other sister Kat and her daughter. Kat and I prayed and I went to Trinity church for service. I received a revelation from God but it was soon lost because I still did not have a place to stay. This situation reminded me of the parable of the sower. *Matthew 13: 21 states that the one who received the seed that fell among the thorns is the person who hears the word, but the worries of this life and the deceitfulness of wealth choke it, making it unfruitful.* My sister, Natalie, would not allow me to stay with her and neither did my best friend Rena. Rena talked to Natalie for me while I was out trying to find a place to stay. At least Rena did give me money. Natalie told Rena that she was tired of the drug use and helping her drug-addicted family. I was hurt because, unlike my other brothers and sisters who used drugs, I had never borrowed money from my sister or asked her for anything. I later learned that, her hard heart was divinely inspired to set me on the path of finding God.

Then Lara, my former lover, finally consented to a few days at her apartment. While there I attended AA meetings nearby. She said that she didn't originally allow me to stay because she knew I was upset with her for talking me into St Josephs' Hospital psych ward. Yes, I was, but I needed a place to stay. I got over the hurt and anger. Being homeless helps one to resolve many issues. As they say in AA, one day at a time. You are never done, and in treatment they remind you to "always leave the door ajar-just a little-so that you can see how far you've come." *The twelve steps taught in AA are good, but they leave you hanging. The reason being is because they are government-funded. They cannot identify any God. They tell you that you could not manage your life and that you must turn your life over to a higher power. They must stop there, in order not to offend anyone. The good part is that they let you know you need God. The bad part is they can't say what God. That leaves the hurting person prey to any type of religion and God (7).*

One Saturday I came to our house, with Kevin's permission, to pick up more of my things and I used the telephone to call my sister Rhoda. She told me that I could move in with her. She informed me that she had helped some of my other siblings that could not acquire help from other family members. One such person was my brother, Bug, the one who died in the hotel room. The one my father kicked out after finding out that he was gay.

I paid Rhoda rent from the disability check I received. When I was admitted to St Josephs Hospital, I was able to apply for disability and receive a check from my employer. The people I thought would help did not. Although Rhoda was like a mother to me when I was a toddler, she was not that way to me as an adult. Remember we would get high together. She had stopped getting high some years prior to this incident. She moved to South Holland with her daughter and grandchildren. I slept on a couch bed in her living room. I became close to her grandchildren too.

On a Friday Summer night, I went to Chicken's house to get high. Kevin and his friends were upstairs playing their usual mind games with me so I left Chicken's and went down the street to another person's house. A woman entered from the rear of the apartment, I had seen her before at a nearby bar. I first saw this woman when I was still living with Kevin. I went to the bar to buy drugs. Side bar: when I left the bar that night I noticed a van parked down the street that resembled Kevin's. I didn't check it out because I was rushing back home to get high. Now back to the drug house. I offered this woman some drugs and she told me in a snappy tone that she only smokes weed. I said, "Good for you". She had a very angry spirit directed toward me. She left the room and returned to a rear bedroom. I started to see things. There was a floor length mirror located where I could see who was in the back of the apartment and they could see me. I thought I saw Kevin. This freaked me out. I kept feeling something pulling on me, going into my pockets where I had my money. I did not see any hands but I felt the hands. A lady asked me to buy her a pipe and I sold her mine then I left the apartment and drove back to Rhoda's house. I was exhausted and almost fell asleep several times. I also got lost. Upon arriving to her house, she let me in. I was so happy to arrive safely, I started to cry. I told her what happened that night. She told me not to go back to Chicken's house and that he is not to be trusted. I slept for a few hours and awakened to go to Kevin's place, to get money, my TV and other things from the house. When I got to the house, he let me in and I accused him of stealing from me or having his friends do it. He told me that I was crazy. I put my TV into the back of my truck with some other items that belonged to him as payment for money taken from me. He told me that I was not going to take those items. I grabbed a knife, he grabbed me and took the knife from my hand and said to someone I could not see, "she's strong". After retrieving the knife he bruised me pretty badly then left the house. I called my sister Natalie's house to tell her what happened. She was not at home so I told my nephew. As I was getting into my truck, Kevin returned with his friend, a policeman. I would not get out of my truck and told the policeman to shoot me. I was then removed from the truck, handcuffed and arrested because I violated the order of protection. My truck keys were given to Kevin and my truck remained in his driveway. I showed the police my bruises and told them that Kevin should be arrested.

Once at the station, I was finger printed, booked, driven to a lock up facility, and placed in a cell with other women. I called my family, collect on a pay phone inside of the cell, asking to be bailed out but none provided assistance. I waited until Monday for bail to be set by the court. The crazy part is, I had the money to bail myself out but it was money I planned to get high with. You see how faulty my thinking was? Then Rhoda's daughter obtained some money and bailed me out. She picked up my nephew who reclaimed my vehicle from Kevin and they both came to pick me up. I drove my truck back to Rhoda's house and noticed that Kevin had taken the items that were his from the back of the truck. When I arrived at my sister's house I bathed and went out to get high. I paid my niece the money she used to bail me out when I received my next check.

I learned prisons/jails do not rehabilitate. I also learned how to murder a person and get off scott free. I was told that since my husband was trying to declare me insane, I would not spend time in prison for killing him. For a moment I thought about allowing the crazy label to stick.

I was arrested before dark so I was fortunate enough to get a mat that I placed on the concrete bed, instead of sleeping on the floor. There were blankets that were needed, in summer, because the air conditioning was set high. The washroom had no door and everyone could hear and see you doing your business. The room smelled bad too. As for the food, homeless people have better. I met many women who had been arrested for defending themselves from abusive men. Drug use was involved in every case.

Court day came and we were all lined up in a hallway and listened to each person's case. No privacy here either. At the hearing, about a month later, I received the bail money paid. I was angry and hurt and felt betrayed by this experience which fed the desire to do more drugs. *The enemy beats you with hopelessness, guilt, shame, depression, and condemnation. You are that hamster in the cage. You run around in that same inescapable circle (11).*

While I stayed with Rhoda, my daughter, Shell, and I were not communicating. Kevin received a check endorsed in both our names from the Trustee of the bankruptcy we applied for but cancelled the process. Kevin cashed it. I thought she helped him cash the check and I told her that I was notifying the authorities that I did not sign the check. She became upset and called me a "hype bitch". That phrase made it hard for me to speak to her. She was just expressing her anger about the hurt I caused her. There was also some un-resolved anger from the incident that happened at Rhoda's house when she was spending the night there at the age of five. You may remember the story of how she cut her neck and my sister did not know how it happened. Well, the truth came out over fifteen years later. I learned that my brother-in-law, Chicken, the one, I've been getting high with, had molested her. She was upset because I was getting high with the person who violated her. You see how things work out, if I had never gotten high, I may have never discovered what happened to my daughter. Fear kept her quiet until she saw how the information could possibly stop me from using. I guess that's one way to look at it. Once a person gets high and everyone knows it, the person has to build the trust that was lost in the substance-abuse process. I eventually stopped going to Chicken's place but I did not stop getting high.

Chapter 8

Ronnie

I'm still living with my sister, who was married to Chicken, the man whose house I would visit to get high. One Saturday night during the summer, I went to Chicken's house to get high. I was on my last hit of drugs, when Tiny came into the house with a tall black drink of water. This was the first time I laid eyes on Ronald Butler. She saw him at the cash station and noticed that he could not retrieve his funds. Tiny told him that she had a friend that worked at a bank that could help him. He followed her back to the house. He saw me getting high and asked for a hit. He said "I will give it back to you when I'm able to get my money". Then he showed me his deposit slips and said, "I have money in the bank, I just can't get to it". I told him that after midnight he would be able to withdraw more money. I gave him a hit. Later, I washed my face, brushed my teeth, and drove him to the cash station. He gave me his cash station card and his pin number. I withdrew the funds and gave him the money, his card, and receipt. This man kissed me and I felt like I was flying. Remember, I had been getting high. I told Ron to be careful around Chicken and Tiny with his money but he had very good discernment of spirits back then. We hit it off; we both had been thrown out of our homes by our spouses for drug use. We both had the same kind of spirit living in us. Ron was living in a shelter and was concerned that he would have no place to stay because he missed curfew that night. The next morning, I let him use my cell phone to save his spot. He was shocked that I allowed him to do that. Why not? We had just had wild passionate sex the night before; the least I could do was let him use my cell phone after letting him use my body. We bathed and went to get something to eat and then I drove him to the shelter.

Ron called me daily. I would pick him up from the shelter and we would go riding. During these excursions, we would talk and get something to eat, and then I would drop him off at work. He was working for SAMs club, during this time. We vowed to stop getting high. We were having a good time together without drugs.

Ron and I would travel to Wisconsin on weekends. I moved from Rhoda's house and rented an apartment in Joliet. We decided to move in together which also coincided with me returning to work at the ITT campus that Kevin was attending. The Friday we were to combine our money, to pay for the apartment deposit, Ron called and said "come and get my money". I told him to hold it. I was tired and did not want to drive back to Chicago, my mistake, because he got high. He had been laid off from SAMs and was upset, a trigger. *The addictive demon was only lying dormant. Until there is deliverance, there can be only short-term change. How many times does the addict swear they will not use again, often with tears in their eyes? They mean it when they say it, but when that controlling spirit rises up they do it again. These persons have no control over that spirit than a person with a compulsive eating disorder (8).* He finally called my sister's house and I went to retrieve him from Chicago. He told me that he was no good for me and that I should give up on him. I did not listen to him; I told him that I could not treat a person like I was treated. I could not throw him away for being weak. He was very happy about this. Thank God I did not depend on his money to get the place. We rented a truck and he encouraged some guys from the shelter to help us move.

Our first destination was the storage unit that Kevin had stored the items from the house once he was foreclosed and evicted. He put me out and still did not keep the house.

I'm back at work and Ron is at home. He cooks dinner and cleans the apartment for me. Our relationship was working well. Ron fought to receive unemployment. He was an experienced liar and smooth talker. He could accomplish anything, once his mind was made up. He was awarded his unemployment. Ron would call me during my breaks and we talked about how I was fairing working around Kevin. I would return home from work to peace and a happy man.

One Friday, I gave my students an exam as I always did, Kevin walks into the classroom. He said that he wanted to speak to one of my students. I told him that I had a fiancé and was moving on with my life. Of course, he tried to play it off. His intrusion into my classroom was just the justification I needed to buy drugs. That night, I bought drugs into the new apartment and Ron and I got high.

This was the beginning of our demise. We fussed and fought on a regular basis after the intrusion of the demonic substance re-surfaced. I often called into work sick. I did not want to see Kevin. Of course my boss was not happy with me calling in sick. I became depressed because of drug use. One night after getting high, Ron developed bumps on his body. I took him to the hospital and they gave him Benadryl. I told him that he needed to stop using drugs. That experience did not stop him.

I would send Ron to purchase drugs in my truck. He would not return until he used all the drugs, this is one incident that caused distrust in our relationship. I had to go everywhere with him in my truck.

Michelle was pregnant with Dorian, my grandson, and she obtained my telephone number. Remember we were not speaking because she called me a "hype bitch". She invited me to her baby shower. I wanted Ron to go but we had been getting high the night before. I attended and Kevin and his family were there. I wished Ron could have been there. I told Ron that Kevin attended the shower and that he should have attended. After getting some rest, he agreed. Shell tried to visit a few times but we were getting high and did not want to stop for company, not even my daughter. Plus I did not want her to see that I was still getting high.

The first thing I needed to do was build a strong relationship with God. The next thing was to stop using drugs and work on rebuilding the broken pieces of my relationship with my daughter. If I couldn't have a relationship with her, nothing would be right.

I re-applied for disability because of depression. It took more than a month for the denial determination and we were behind in our rent. Ron's unemployment check did not cover the rent. We sold everything in the apartment which was not enough to pay rent and we were evicted. I bought a ticket to Mississippi for Ron. He would be staying with his friend George that he was always talking about. My daughter allowed me to move in with her. While living with her and Ron out of town, I did not do drugs but I did not throw away my pipe. I was not ready to be set free.

December 10th Shell went into labor, there was a snow storm. She wanted me to drive her car instead of my truck, the Ford Explorer whose brakes were not the best. I was not accustom to driving a non-four-wheel-drive automobile, especially in the snow. We drove onto Highway 55 and the car started to fish tail. The car turned completely around in the opposite direction. I know I cried out to God. This happened during rush hour and no cars struck us. I straightened the car and drove her to the hospital. She almost had the baby in the car on the highway.

Ron and I called each other regularly. I planned to meet him in Mississippi. I officially resigned from ITT in Jan 2001 and waited for my last check to leave Illinois. I was able to take the truck into the automotive school Shell worked for to get the brakes repaired for the price of parts. I asked Ron to assist with driving to Mississippi (MS). I bought him a bus ticket and he returned to Illinois (IL). He was kind of strung out when he arrived in Illinois. He told me that he had been drinking. From experience, I knew that he had done more but I did not press the issue. As we were leaving Illinois, I threw the pipe; I had in the glove compartment, into the dumpster.

Ron drives all the way to Hattiesburg, Mississippi. It was snowing when we left Illinois but the weather in Mississippi was beautiful for February. I did not expect to see so many pine trees. We arrived at his friend George's house. We lived in the servant's quarters of the house. This little apartment was connected to the garage. It had a living room, dining area/kitchen and bedroom with connecting bath. We did not have a bed, so pillows were placed on the floor as a make shift bed. I did not feel comfortable sleeping on the floor so the chair I bought from Illinois was taken into the apartment to sleep on. Ron would sleep on the couch. We would only go to the pallet to have sex. It was not much of that going on there. Ron would go out walking and I thought he was visiting someone. He was; he went to visit his daughter who lived down the street. He finally introduced me to his daughter and her mother. Even though the mother had a boyfriend, she still had a thing for Ronnie.

We started looking for work. I filled out applications at several schools and manufacturing plants. We did not own a telephone but we used George's telephone as a means of contact. George did not give us the messages from employers who called. We discovered this when calling the employers to ask if the positions had been filled. I don't know why George did not give us the messages. Ron surmised that it was childhood jealousy going on between them.

Ron was the first to find employment, working for the county of Hattiesburg. They actually allowed a person to start work before their drug test results were received. When Ron came to Illinois to help me drive to Mississippi, he had gotten high at one of the rest stops. I discovered that he had been getting high in Mississippi too. I would drive Ron to work and go to the library to search on line for jobs. Ron worked until his drug test results came back positive. He was fired. He again applied for unemployment. We were also looking for an apartment. Before leaving Illinois I filed income tax, and asked Shell to send the check to me, once it arrived. She asked to borrow some of it.

Ron informed me that George required that we pay him a certain amount for rent. I gave him that amount to give to George. Then George came back and tried to acquire more. I then went directly to his wife and told her the game her husband was trying to play with me. She was not aware of any cash arrangement between him and Ronnie. I did not relinquish more than Ron told me prior to receiving my funds.

I also got high in Mississippi. Ron borrowed my truck to go out with George and he did not return until later that night and the truck had a flat tire. He had been in the quarters, a bad section in Hattiesburg, getting high. I told him that he could not use the truck and to change the flat. He was out of it, tired from the all nighter but he did get up and fix the flat. Since I was not going to let him use the truck alone, he took me to get high at one of his other friends' house.

One weekend he went out with George and I went to this other friend's house. When he returned home I was not there, so he started to look for me. He saw my truck as he was walking toward this friend's house. He was upset with me. When we returned home he told me that he was going to put me out. I again talked to the woman of the house and asked if she wanted me to leave and she told me that Ronnie could not put me out of her house. He finally calmed down but I was not going to just sit in the house while he did his thing. You see, I could have done something else without using drugs but I had no control. Ron was the only person I knew in Mississippi until he introduced me to his friends.

I could not find a job in Hattiesburg, my girlfriend from Chicago, Rena, suggested Las Vegas. I had nothing to lose and much to gain so we planned to leave Mississippi by the end of March 2001. Prior to our leaving Ron would work temp jobs to obtain money for food. George's wife would invite us to dinner but that was growing old. Since I had gone to George's wife about the game he was trying to play on me, he did not want us in his house.

George was Ron's last resort. His family would not allow him to live with them. Ron's sister took one look at him and asked was he on drugs. She surmised this because his skin tone was dark. Of course, Ron said no. I met his brothers while in Mississippi. Ron's family rejected him as some of my family had done to me. Ron showed me the neighborhood he grew up in and told of how it changed.

We started getting high regularly. We would get high while driving in the truck, or go to another one of his friend's house, to do the same. I informed Ron of my plan to move to Las Vegas and he agreed. We planned to pool the money that Shell owed me with his unemployment check and drive to Vegas.

Thank God the day came to leave George's house. George did not think we would move. But I was going to get out of his place one way or another. Before heading to Vegas I talked to Leonard Watts, our landlord when I was a kid on California Ave in Chicago, via telephone, who lives in Vegas. We planned to meet him and his daughter once we arrived in town.

We got a flat tire in New Orleans, on a rode where very few motorists traveled. A truck stopped to help and drove us to a gas station and then to a tire shop. We did not have enough money for the tire and Shell had to wire the money she owned me to buy the tire. The tire shop attendant drove us to Kmart to pick up the wire transfer. Ron and

I were amazed by how God was moving in this situation. We also stopped in Texas and visited my youngest sister Jackie. She offered us her apartment to stay the night. She was planning to spend the night at her girlfriend's house. I don't know why we didn't take her up on her offer because we could not afford a hotel. But we checked into a hotel and slept until morning and headed toward Vegas again. We argued most of the time during this trip. We were tired and having withdrawals.

We finally arrived in Vegas and checked into the Golden Spike hotel. Again we started our job search routine. Our money was running low. Ron was the first to find employment. He told me that he never had a problem finding a job. He was correct on that fact. He was a hard worker and skilled laborer. When we did not have enough money for the hotel, Leonard allowed us to stay in his mobile home. It had a kitchen with dining area, a bedroom, and a sitting area. They even let us borrow their TV and also paid the rental fee at the trailer park.

The job Ron obtained was working with concrete. I would drive him to work and then go to the employment office to search for work. I re-designed my resume and sent them out. I went on several interviews but Vegas is a closed town for those who were not permanent residence. So I got a Las Vegas license and that helped because I was hired and started training for a telecommunications position. Upon completion of the training, I was transferred to their Boulder Hwy office.

One morning, while still living in the mobile home, Ron drove my truck to the store to buy fish and did not return. When Ron wanted to get high he would start an argument with me so I would put him out and he could justify getting high because he was put out. This time there was no argument and I reported the truck stolen. I gave the police a description of Ron and they found him walking the streets near downtown Vegas. They drove him to a shelter and he told them that he had been carjacked. During this time frame I was not getting high and thank God, his actions did not trigger me.

Later that day I was visited Leonard and his daughter. During my visit a woman called and informed me that my truck was parked in front of her house with the keys in the door. Leonard's phone number was written on some paper in the glove compartment. Leonard and his daughter Deb drove me to retrieve the truck and gave me a few bucks to give to the woman. I had to call the police so they could process the truck to take it off the stolen car list. Someone had taken the truck into the desert; they walked or danced on the hood and left dirty underwear in a bag in the back seat. I think they were Ron's.

About a week later, I was driving down the Las Vegas stripe toward the library, and low and behold, guess who I saw walking down the streets? Something had, (The Holy Spirit) told me that I would see him. Ron flagged me down. I pulled over, he seemed happy that I had the truck. He tried to tell me again that he was carjacked. I told him, "don't go there, I talked to the people you were with". I also told him that was how I got the truck back. Ron wanted to leave the shelter he was living in. He later found a half-way house and moved in. He was embarrassed to return to the mobile home. He did not want to risk seeing Leonard and Deb. It seemed that he had more concern about what they thought of him than me. The guy who operated the half-way house informed me that Ron needed to stay there for a while. I told him that it was fine with me. Then Ron changed his mind about staying there.

The mobile home park was far from my job and I needed to find a place closer to work. I shared with my boss at the Telecommunication Company that I was homeless and she took up a collection for me to stay in a hotel. They collected enough money for me to stay in a hotel for a week. I again stayed in the Golden Spike until I received my first paycheck and some money from Ron. I use the money to rent an apartment down the street from my job. Of course, Ron moved in. The apartments were called the La Palomino Apartments. Although Ron helped with the deposit I did not put him on the lease. During the credit check process I discovered that the lawyers Kevin and I hired to file bankruptcy back in Illinois had filed without complete payment for the services or directions from us to proceed. Thank God, this did not stop me from renting the apartment. Ron helped with purchasing a bed too. We tied it to the top of the truck to bring it home. We also purchased a television and bar stools from the Goodwill. We were fine until we started using drugs again.

Many things happened while living in this apartment. One being; Ron and I would physically fight, most caused by our getting high. He would push me down or try to choke me. I gave him a run for his money. I fought back but did not leave. I guess I learned that from seeing abuse in my family.

Trust was still a problem in our relationship. I always thought that when I was at work, he had someone in the house. As I look back on this I can't believe that I allowed myself to get in this type of situation. But when you are addicted to a demonic substance, you experience many things that you would not do under "normal" conditions.

All the choices I made for my life that I thought would save it were killing me. At times I felt like there were other beings living inside me and I was not in control of them. The many years of drug use aided in these feelings.

Ron was injured while at work. As he was working with a machine that inserts bolts into concrete forms; a bolt cut his finger through to the bone. He was probably talking to someone and/or working fast. He was required to have physical therapy to gain mobility. I would drive Ron to and from therapy. The day of the injury, on the way home from the clinic we bought drugs. He became upset with me because I had more drugs left over out of my share when he had finished his. I would not share so he tried to hit me. Remember, this man had just cut his finger. I grabbed his finger and told him that he better not try to hit me. He screamed. I finally let go but he got mad and pushed me down on the way out of the door. Of course, I let him return, later.

Ron decided to hired a lawyer to sue the company but nothing came of that except the lawyer's assistant trying to hook up with him. One such incident occurred when we went to tell the lawyer that we were leaving Vegas. The assistant asked Ron, "Do you really want to leave?" This really made me think that they had gotten together. Ron just sat in the chair and was speechless, which is not like him. I finally said, "Ron, tell her that you want to leave." Then he finally said "yes, I want to leave". I questioned him about that incident but he said I was just paranoid and insecure. That was his typical answer when I would be close to the truth.

Ron and I would argue and he would threaten me and I'd call the police. He would leave and I would let him back in. This was a regular event for us. The company that Ron worked for required him to be on site to receive a disability check. I would also drive him to and from this office daily. One time when I called the police and put Ron out, the following day I went to fill out a police report. The detectives came to the apartment to arrest him but he was at the office for disability duty and I did not tell them where he worked so he could be arrested. As you can see, I did not know what I was doing. I'm getting ahead of myself.

Now back to my job at the Telecommunication Company, I worked in a large warehouse size room with many other people. We wore headsets and sold telecommunication services over the telephone. The sale calls were automatically generated. The only time we stopped was to go to the bathroom or lunch. The employees were required to sell a certain quota each week and I did not reach the sell quota and was laid off. I applied for unemployment. Before I lost my job we started going to church and bible study. I've discovered that when you are in sin and try to change your life, Satan turns up the heat to get you back on the sin track.

One incident took us back to that life. It took a great deal of time before I received the first unemployment check. We were evicted from another apartment. But before we left we sold everything like we did in Illinois and tried to get a room but did not obtain enough money from the items we sold. Also Ron's disability check was not large enough to pay the rent but it could have gotten us a room but we wanted to get high. It would seem that the past circumstances should have taught us that drugs use was the wrong choice but we gave in to the temptation. *That demonic controlling spirit rose up again. Until there is deliverance, there can only be short-term change (9).* We still looked for work and found that there was work in Minnesota, (MN). I did not want to go to MN because it's cold there. I wanted to live in a warmer climate but not Vegas or Mississippi. My oldest sister Enid, whom we call Day-Day, wired me money for a hotel room.

The hotel my sister helped us acquire was not the best but we were not living on the streets. It even had a refrigerator and microwave.

I allowed Ron to use the truck to go somewhere, maybe to his doctor's appointment, or even to buy drugs, I don't remember now, but I was laying in bed watching a Christian program on TV. The guy was explaining Jesus' crucifixion. His description was surreal; I could feel Jesus' pain. I was totally convicted and I told Ron about it when he returned. We also got high while living in this hotel but not that night. I prayed a lot in Vegas. I can honestly say that I had been praying even before I left Illinois. I did attend church, Trinity, occasionally while in Illinois.

My unemployment check finally came and I found another hotel room in a better location. This place had a dining area, kitchen with stove and refrigerator, and a couch in the living room. This place was a one-bedroom apartment for most. There were families living in this facility. We did not get high there, but we argued and Ron itched. Ron also broke out in hives while in Vegas. I thought it was the drug reaction or withdrawal.

We left Vegas and headed to Minnesota. I spoke to headhunters from Minnesota and set up appointments for when we arrived in town. Minnesota was the one place that had the most amounts of jobs available. Ron had been talking about going to Minnesota since I first met him. The check that would take us out of Vegas was less than $700 and arrived the afternoon of Aug, 2001. We cashed it at a casino and headed out of town.

In Denver Colorado, we stopped and bought drugs. This was not very wise to get high in a town that we knew nothing about, but we were not thinking straight. This is just another example how God kept us even in our mess. As you can see, Ron could find drugs anywhere. After this incident we vowed not to do that again. We stopped at Wal-mart, as always, Ron spoke to the locals and they asked if we were moving to town. Ron and I laughed at that question because we did not see any blacks in town, at least not at the Wal-mart. We spent one night at a hotel in this small town (majority white) I don't remember the name of it, and then headed to Minnesota.

Chapter 9

Starting Over

As we were nearing Minnesota we stopped at a gas station to ask for directions. Ron wanted to go to Minneapolis and I wanted to go to St Paul. We decided to go to St Paul. We stayed in a hotel near the Mystic Lake casino. We thought that the casino hotel would be inexpensive like the hotels in Vegas but they were not. The next day we called the human services office and headed to downtown St Paul. We checked out some other hotels but they were not in our budget either. I feared we were going to have to stay in a shelter. We had less than $200. We found ourselves at the Dorothy Day Center shelter. There was a waiting list for spaces. We had another argument and I did not want to stay in a shelter. I put Ron out of the truck again and started to head back to Illinois. But the Holy Spirit stopped me. I really didn't want to go back and live with my daughter. I went back to Dorothy Day and found Ron and told him that I would rather sleep in the truck instead of a shelter. We had to use the washroom, so we went to the hospital around the corner from the Dorothy Day center. We were also told that we could use the telephone free there. We made some phone calls to organizations to inquire about assistance. While I was in the washroom, Ron was talking to an elder man by the name of Walter Carry. Ron told him about our situation. The man said that he had an apartment that he rarely used and was trying to get out of the lease. He said that we could use his place. We followed him in the Ford Explorer that took us from Illinois to Mississippi to Nevada and finally to Minnesota. We followed him to the Salvation Army to make arrangements to get food.

Mr. Carry had a one-bedroom apartment near Maryland Ave on Westminster in St Paul. I wondered where we were going to sleep, it turned out that his couch was a queen size bed and we had queen size sheets. We promised to pay Mr. Carry when my unemployment check came or when we found work, which ever came first. The next morning we started looking for work again. We registered with the employment office, and I rented a PO Box so I could receive my unemployment check. We bought food and gave Mr. Carry a few bucks. While at the employment office, we printed several job sheets. I faxed resumes to some and we called a few. There was one job that Ron seemed not to notice. I pointed it out to him and asked him to check it out. He called Bonestro Engineering and they asked him to come in for an interview. The secretary gave me directions and we went to the interview. The interviewer invited me into the room with Ron. I gave him my resume and he gave me a book of engineering firms in the twin cities. Ron was hired on the spot. He had to take a physical and pass a drug test, which he was able to do because we had not gotten high since Colorado.

Early in the morning, I drove Ron to work. Then, I would head to the employment office to look for a job. I would then return to the apartment to cook dinner and later pick him up from work. I also prayed a lot. We were not on the streets but we still did not know Mr. Carry from Adam. Then things started to get crazy. You know, addicts have a pattern they go through; when they have money. They try to justify why they must spend it. If they don't buy drugs they become upset. Most deny they are really craving the drug. This is what would happen when Ron got paid. We would argue but Ron did not hit me, then.

Ron smoked cigarettes and he would leave the apartment to smoke. I did not trust him to do that, because when he returned he would act strangely like he was high. That would really freak me out. He probably was high from the cigarettes. He did not smoke regularly, because we did not have money to buy cigarettes. We would argue about this and he would tell me how insecure I was. I now know there was insecurity but I had good reason to be insecure about my relationship with him.

The following scenario shows one reason why I was insecure: While in Vegas, I felt that Ron was or had an affair, so I told him that my doctor suggested that I get tested to determine what kind of infection I had. I did not realize that it was the Holy Spirit telling me to go to the clinic and bring what was done in the dark to light. Ron accompanied me to the clinic and I told him to get checked to ensure that he did not have the same infection and to get some medicine. While in the doctor's office, I told the nurse that I wanted to be tested for a sexually transmitted disease. He asked was I using protection, I told him no and that I had only one sex partner who was waiting to be examined. The nurse put Ron in a room and tested him. It was discovered that he did have a sexually transmitted disease. The nurse convinced him to tell me. He came into my examining room and his eyes were red as if he was crying. He told me the situation and then said that he must have gotten it from his wife. I was very surprised that I did not get upset but was happy that my suspicions were confirmed. We were both given medication and condoms. Now the awesome part is that I did not have it, but I did take the medication just in case. I would tell Ron, when I became upset with him, that he gave me a sexually transmitted disease and tried to say that he caught it from his wife; whom he had been separated from for over six months.

Remember, when we were in Illinois I had taken Ron to the hospital for a rash? He was given many blood tests to diagnose the cause of the rash and they did not find a sexually transmitted disease until Vegas, so you see, trust was not a strong suit in our relationship. Now I know the rash was from his liver's inability to rid itself of impurities in the drugs he was using. I also learned that STDs like syphilis and gonorrhea could hide in your body and when tested, the results don't always come back positive. This whole process of distrust and arguing continued. Then Mr. Carry tried to run a game on us and try to extort more money than what was originally agreed upon. But I kept on praying.

My relationship with Ron got worst. Ron threatened me and I had visions of our fights in Vegas. The next day after dropping him off at work I called a battered woman's shelter. I was referred to Woman's Advocate on Grand Ave in St Paul. I set up an appointment, interviewed, and was accepted. While Ron was at work, I returned to Mr. Carry's apartment to get my things. I was not able to take everything. I came back later and tried to talk to Ron. He was in the tub and he wanted me to wash his back, imagine that. I asked if we could talk but he did not want to talk. I gathered the rest of my things and started to leave when he threatened to kill me and called me all sorts of terrible names. I was happy that I made the decision to leave. This was in September 2001 after 911. While at the shelter I gained confidence, strength, and more clean time. Now isn't that funny, when we first came to town, I didn't want to stay in a shelter but a shelter was really what I needed. Ron would call me on a cell phone he purchased for me. I did not tell him where I was staying. I had to get my life together, stop using drugs, and eventually forgive him. Forgiveness is an important key in life. Without it, all the old feelings of hatred, frustration, bitterness, and anger comes forth like a flood, and along with them comes their partners, defeat and low-self-esteem. Once you forgive, do you ever get rid of the pain? I don't know, but you receive healing. You receive freedom beyond what you thought possible, but I don't know if you totally get rid of the pain. Before I met Jesus, I silenced my pain with drugs, alcohol, work, or sexual misconduct which, in the long run, only served to make the pain worse. Even in my happiest moments, the pain was there waiting for the mere suggestion of rejection to bring it rushing in, reaffirming all the negative feelings I had ever had about myself. In those times of weakness, suicide seemed to be the only solution. I knew for certain that a sound mind cannot exist with deep unforgiveness and rage. There is a direct tie between forgiveness and wholeness.

None of us like pain, uncertainty, strife, or frustration. We want things to run smoothly. But the challenging and miserable times are not without their aspect of good. Things happen to us during those times that are as precious as gold. For it is then that we have the opportunity to experience the Lord's presence in a deeper way. If we embrace the moment, we see Him in it. Have you ever found yourself angry, upset, or devastated when things didn't turn out as you'd hoped or planned? Next time that happens, look deeply into the situation and ask God to give you a new perspective.

Saying Yes to God is another key. Everything I desired of God to be implanted in me couldn't happen until I let my own life go. I joined the River of Life church which was located down the street from the shelter. Ron found a church too, a Lutheran church across from Regions hospital. He told me that it was a recovery church and he was the only black there. Ron noticed a difference in me. While I was in the shelter Ron bought a car from a co-worker. This was good so he did not have to ride the bus or pay Mr. Carry to drive him to work. One Saturday I went to the apartment to visit him and he was not there. I just knew he was out with someone getting high. So I got a hotel room and got high. I later discovered that he was doing the same. I returned to the shelter before curfew, which did not cause suspicion for a drug test. When Ron finally called me he was depressed and talking about suicide. I could not leave the shelter, thank God, so I called an ambulance to take him to the hospital. He was released the following morning and I went to visit him at Mr. Carry's apartment. We talked about our relationship and how drugs destroyed it. We again vowed to never use drugs. Ron still did not know that I was staying in a shelter. While at the shelter I also started the divorce process from Kevin. I started to search for an apartment too. The shelter helped with the deposit but I had to find a place that would accept bad credit and no rental history in Minnesota. With Ron's help, I found the La Blanche apartment on Western Ave. He told me a guy he met on the bus informed him about the apartments. I checked it out and we filled out an application. Tracy the apartment manager was very helpful in getting us in. We moved in Oct. 30, 2001. The shelter gave me a furniture voucher. I then started attending the Lutheran church with Ron. Things were going good for a while and then we started to use again. *No matter how many times the addict swear they will not use again, until there is deliverance, there is only short-term change (10).* This of course caused more problems, and more distrust.

I continued to drive Ron to and from work. He would complain about me not working. He said I was lazy and did not want to work. Everyday after dropping him off, I would go to the employment office and send out resumes for jobs. I had a few interviews but nothing came from them. Some mornings I would drop him off at work, withdraw money from the bank account, and buy drugs after leaving the employment office. Then I would return home, get high, until it was time to pick him up. I did not share this fact with him. Until, one day I was getting high, I got so high I did not feel safe driving. I finally came down enough to drive and I drove to his job but he had left. I found him walking, I don't know how, except I was being guided to him. That same day we had an appointment for counseling with Pastor

Joe, of the Lutheran recovery church. We called and cancelled and continued to get high.

With continued drug use, Ron had become more agitated and would threaten me. I would tell him to leave, call the police, then let him back in. This was the dance we did. When Ron would get paid he would start a fight so he could use. And I would get upset that he used and I would use. Ron's job at Bonestro was seasonal and he was laid off in Nov. He started receiving unemployment soon after. If I did not accompany him to cash his check, he would go out and use and we would not have money for food or gas.

Ron would make comments about me being a dike/gay and that the only thing I could do well was give head (oral sex). Bad choice of words for him, for I said, "You will never get oral sex from me again!" I told him that if he did not like me he could leave. He would tell me that he was not going and that I was crazy, another wrong word. I was still traumatized by Kevin attempts to have me committed and declared insane. I told him that he was also crazy for staying with someone he knew was crazy.

Chapter 10

Deliverance, Restoration and Promotion

One day after getting high and arguing about nothing in particular, Ron got upset and started to choke me. I remember having a feeling of peace come over me and I was willing to die just to get away. He saw the look on my face and stopped. I knew from that moment on I would never get high again.

With this major deliverance, I thought, taken care of; God could begin His cleanup program on me. Excess baggage had to be eliminated, the major of which was self. All my desires to be noticed, to be somebody, to do something great had to be given up to Him. My dreams had to be His dreams, the ones He placed in my heart. They couldn't be the ones I thought I should have, or needed for the purpose of making people like me. "Okay, Lord," I finally said, "I give up my desires to be anyone important or to do anything significant. I will no longer regard not being a success in the world's eyes as a failure, because you love me the way I am. The death process, of "self", was long and painful. In the early days of deliverance, I still had dreams about drugs. I'd dream about getting high. I would be with the old crowd and thinking, "If I could just have a little bit…no one would know." And then this voice would say, "God will know." At that moment I would start talking to the people present in the dream about God and what He had done in my life. The fact that I didn't get to the drugs, even in my dreams, was a statement to me of my determination to stay clean. Every recovering addict has "drug dreams" in one form or another.

In the interim Ron and I discovered that there was a black church that shared the Lutheran church we were attending. The name of the church is Berean. We first saw Berean's children's choir at the Lutheran's church Christmas program. Ron approached the Pastor of Berean and asked him, "When is your service?" We then started attending Berean's service at 12:30. On New Years Eve we were attending church at Berean.

Ron was still having problems with his skin breaking out and itching. We went to the health department for treatment and they prescribed medicine for scabies without confirmation of infection. But we applied the medicine and went to the New Years Eve service. The medicine did not work because he did not have scabies. I'm sure now that the medicine even aggravated Ron's liver problem. In February 2002, I was hired at Wal-Mart. A month after my unemployment stopped and three months after I stopped using drugs.

Ron was still receiving unemployment and would cash his check and use. He would return home, after using crack, beat down. I took his mailbox key but that did not work because he would wait for the mail lady and get his check from her. Ron had the ability to talk women into doing things they would not normally do. Lack of trust was still an issue within our relationship. When I would go to work I would wonder if when I returned home, the things that were there when I left would still be there when I returned. One good thing, Ron did not steal. We still argued a lot. I prayed and prayed and kept a journal, which aided in writing this book. Again, I would put him out, call the police, and I even called the Pastor. But prayer was the only thing that worked for me to keep me straight and drug free. I had to pray daily for

God's strength to overcome the temptation to use drugs because Ron was still using.

I submitted my resume to the railroad for a dispatcher's position and was called about another position, Communications Maintainer. I was asked to interview. This was also in February 2002. I was interviewed by Mr. Byers. My maiden name is Byars. I felt this was confirmation that I was going to get the job. I was hired and started working on March 4th 2002. As a matter of fact, my divorce from Kevin was final then too. It was not easy getting the job. Satan was on the attack. I passed the physical and because I could not squat to the floor, the doctor said I would not be able to perform the job. I told the doctor that squatting would not be part of my duties and I asked Mr. Byers to confirm this. I prayed to God and he touched the doctor's heart who gave permission for Canadian Pacific Railroad, CPR to hire me. I testified about this in church. I went from having no job to having two jobs.

Wal-Mart was the hardest job I ever had. The store was newly built and we had to set up the whole store, install and stock shelves. I eventually stopped working for Wal-mart. Even with these blessings the devil did not rest. Ron received his next unemployment check and again went out to get high. He was gone for more than 24 hours. I got the locks changed so he could not come into the apartment while I was at work but later I let him back in. The next day, I called the Pastor to ask for assistance in putting Ron out. The Pastor called the police but the police would not remove him. The Pastor tried to talk to him but Ron would not speak to him. Ron hid in the bathroom, imagine that. The Pastor finally spoke to Ron and told him that he loved him and that he would not throw him away. This conversation was the catalyst that aided in Ron's immediate deliverance from drugs.

Of course, the Pastor wanted us to live apart and to stop living in sin. Then Ron started his divorce process. I started looking for another apartment because our lease was going to end soon and I was going to use this opportunity to get free from him. I told Ron of my plan and that I no longer wanted to live in sin. This had to be around August or September. I also wanted to live closer to work. So, Ron and I went on a tour of the Churchill Apartments in downtown Minneapolis, which is down the street from my job, connected by the skyway. The skyway in downtown Minneapolis are overhead, heated or air conditioned, depending on the season, indoor walkways. God blessed me with an apartment at the Churchill and I allowed Ron to move in. This happened around Oct. 25, 2002. Ron's divorce was final soon after. Our credit was still bad. I had to pay one month's rent for deposit. We then had to borrow money to rent a truck, but could not get a truck for the day we wanted. We loaded my truck and moved our belongings. We worked together as a team. But you know; we always worked together in some form or another. All through these events I never stopped praying.

When we moved into the apartment, I reminded Ron again that I did not want to live in sin and we were married on Nov. 4th and our lives got even better.

During one of our arguments, Ron told me that the only thing I could do well was give head (oral sex) and I told him that I would never give him oral sex again. After we married, Ron told me that oral sex was not what God wanted us to do. He said that he respected me as his wife and would not ask me to perform that act on him. I was obedient to my husband. God continued to work on us.

While writing in my journal I discovered the time frame for our clean time and Ron's health concern was not very long, less than a year in fact. Ron thought he was clean for two years but he was not. He was not sure of his dates. Until I wrote this neither was I. God was working on us and has plenty of work for us to do. Satan wanted to kill us and stop our blessings. Those years were not that pleasant, but at least I got through them sober, and that was the most important thing at the time. Most recovering addicts would say that we've been to the other side and have seen the jaws of death. We've looked into the face of despair; we have been to the land of no return. Some of us came back; a lot of us didn't. This is where my gratitude continues to prevail.

Through this process I developed my spirituality. I learned to depend on God, even though emotionally I was pretty shaky. No matter what else happened, I was going to be okay. I stopped using drugs (but it was a daily process for me). Remember Ron's deliverance was immediate. I began to read my bible daily; that's where my strength comes from. The hardest thing for me was to develop trust. This continues to be an issue I pray and work on. Even though I don't trust most people, I trust God and I constantly remind myself that God is my protector and no weapon formed against me will prosper.

Ron developed a rash, for the third time, which caused him to itch. We went to a doctor who prescribed allergy medicine and cortisone cream. That did not work. They tested his blood and found that he had hepatitis C but they said that it would not cause a rash. Ron knew he had the virus, but was told that he could live a long time with it. Yes he could, if he did not drink and use drugs. I was not aware that Ron had hepatitis C until after the test results. He then had scans and X-rays and nothing was found to be the cause of the rash. One dermatologist referred him to a liver specialist.

We went to the liver specialist at Regions Hospital in Oct 2002. She took more blood and scheduled more scans. The blood tests came back with liver functions elevated and the scan showed spots on his liver. The doctor started talking of the possibility that Ron would need a transplant but she wanted to perform a biopsy for confirmation. She also wanted Ron to speak to an oncologist, which is a cancer doctor. We informed our primary care doctor that the liver specialist wanted Ron to have a liver transplant. Dr Lewis, the primary care doctor, said that he would not recommend that Ron have the transplant until his health deteriorated more because the transplant could kill him. This doctor felt that Ron should have the transplant as a last resort. Ron saw the oncologist who scheduled the biopsy for Christmas Eve. Ron was diagnosed with liver cancer right after Christmas. The liver specialist referred him to Fairview Hospital, the U of M Hospital transplant division. There he underwent numerous tests starting January 31, 2003. The last test was on February 19th.

All came back negative for spread of cancer to other parts of his body. God is so good. Instead of losing weight he gained weight. Instead of not being able to work he worked a very laborious job of loading trucks on the midnight shift at Target. Ron did not miss one day of work nor church.

Do you know how it can be living with someone who is going through this? They are not at their best. God delivered him from drugs but not his attitude. But God kept me, and put a guard on my mouth and gave me His patience. God has carried me through coordinating appointments for test and ensuring that insurance would pay for procedures. Looking back on this, I know that God was doing all the work and I was just following or being carried.

I would pray to God, that when a liver was found, let it be on our off days.

Monday, February 24, 2003 was like every other Monday, we were off work. Our off days were Monday and Tuesday. We would go shopping, take a ride and take care of business. Upon returning home from our outing this day, I checked the messages. Ann Kalis, Ron's Transplant Coordinator left a message to get permission to put Ron on the transplant list. I immediately told Ron and started to pray. Ron stated, "This is really going too fast". We had also just returned from his last doctor's appointment. I called Ann to tell her it was ok to put Ron on the list and she informed me that she had put him on the list because she felt I would give her permission to do so. I hung up the telephone and told Ron of my conversation with Ann. Later that evening we planned to attend a concert at Berean. This was the week our church was having convocation. We later decided to get some rest. At 8pm our telephone rang and it was a Dr. Harmon who stated that they had found a liver and that he would call back with more information on what to do to get ready if and when we were to come in. The doctor left his pager and cell number so we could contact him.

Remember I asked God to arrange for the procedure to be performed on our off days and Monday and Tuesday were our off days, as stated earlier. Check that out, we also had the same off days; God is awesome how he orchestrates things. A few hours went by and the doctor called and said they would be testing the liver to see if it was a match. He also gave instructions for Ron, to fast, not eat anything, because he may be admitted that night. I told Ron what the doctor said and again Ron said, "This is going too fast, I don't know if I'm ready". I told him that God is really working and He's ready. At 11pm the doctor called and said to head to the hospital. I got Ron's clothes, toothbrush, and other personal affects together. Ron was in shock. His mind was not ready. We checked into the hospital. A nurse had to withdraw ten tubes of blood prior to the procedure. They had to stick him several times because he was afraid and his fluids were low from the fast. Ron's doctor told us that the liver tested positive for HSV and I told him that we could live with that because we were already living with it.

They said that they did not know of a situation where the spouse/sexual partner contracted the virus. I wanted Ron to live and was not concerned about contracting HSV.

Ron told me, "I don't think I can have this transplant". I reassured him that God was in control. His roommate had also undergone liver surgery because his wife needed a liver. She was on the list for quite awhile without a finding a match. He eventually had to give her a portion of his liver. I then told Ron not to fear, God is working here. God positioned us to see how He was moving in our lives by allowing us to hear the testimony of his roommate.

The Nurses and Techs said they had never heard of anyone being put on the list and called the same day. I told them that they had never seen God work. By 7am on Feb. 25, 2003 Ron was heading into surgery. I went home to rest and to make telephone calls to inform my family of our blessing. I left the TV on the gospel channel as I slept. I was awakened after 2 pm when I heard the TV minister state, "the operation was a success, and the patient lived". I got up and tried to get on-line but my computer would not connect to the Internet. The phone rang and it was my boss asking about my husband. I told him that he was still in surgery. As soon as I hung up the telephone it rang again and it was Ann, Ron's Transplant Coordinator telling me that he was out of surgery and in intensive care. If I were on-line, I would not have received that information until after I got off line and checked my messages. I had a dial-up connection not broadband. God even worked for me to get that call.

    I headed to the hospital and as I enter ICU, Ron is conscience and in severe pain with tubes coming out of every opening in his body and extra holes added for drainage. He opened his eyes and saw me and tried to talk. But he could not because of the tube down his throat and one in his nose. I told him not to talk but to blink his eyes to let me know if he was in pain. He started to blink his eyes very fast. I informed the nurse that he was in pain and began to pray. She medicates him but it did not help. I then told her that he has a high tolerance to drugs and her reply to me was that she can only give what the doctor has prescribed. My response to her was that I have not spoken to the doctors about Ron's surgery. She then pages the doctors for me. I encourage Ron not to speak and to stop biting the breathing tube. The nurse told me to wait for the doctors in the family waiting room. I felt Ron's pain and tears came to my eyes but I kept on praying. In the family waiting room I met other families who were also waiting to see members of their family who had recently had surgery.

Ron's doctors came to the family waiting room. I told them that Ron has a very high tolerance to drugs and that he's in a lot of pain. They give the nurse new directives and Ron gradually starts to relax. I tell Ron to relax as much as possible because it will be painful when it's time to remove the tube. I also told him that I was going to church that night to thank God for the miracles He has done. I leave and head to church and testify to everyone about the miracle God has performed. We had not informed anyone at church of Ron's condition. They were all surprised and joyful to learn of God's miracle in our life. I praised and thanked God. I know that the Holy Ghost came upon me that night. When I returned home, I called the hospital to check on Ron. His nurse asked if I wanted to talk to him. I scream, "THE TUBE IS OUT?" The nurse told me that his breathing tube had been removed. I started to cry and thank God again and talked to Ron. He was not feeling any pain this time because he was properly medicated.

The next morning, I went to the hospital to visit Ron. As I waited outside the room, while the doctor examined him, I heard Ron say to the doctor, "don't tell my wife how soon I will be mobile". He also said to the doctor, "You know, my wife spoils me". I also heard the doctor say that they would be moving Ron from ICU. As the doctor left the room, I entered and told Ron, "I heard everything you told the doctor". The doctor told him that at the rate he's going he will return to work in as little as two weeks. The doctor was only joking with him. Ron tells me he was very tense during the night and the Nurses had to massage his back, arms, and legs. Ron told the Nurses that his wife could massage better. I said, "don't tell them that". I told

Ron what happened at church and returned home to get ready for work. I worked the three to eleven shifts. While at work I called to check on Ron's progress and was informed that he had been taken out of ICU and admitted to the transplant ward. His progress was unheard of, for a transplant patient. But nothing is impossible for God. The next day I visited Ron the doctor removed the bandages from the incision. The incisions looked good. Ron was able to bathe himself and get in and out of bed on his own. He did have pain but that's normal considering the operation. He was not allowed to eat, so he chewed on ice. Ron developed a fever which was reduced with Tylenol. I told him to take it easy. His body clock was off; he'd awake at night and sleep during the day. He missed home and asked to leave daily. I told him that he'll be home soon after his temperature stays down and the need for pain medication decreases. The hospital staff is amazed at his progress, I kept telling them it's God doing His work. Ron became a new man. I guess being close to death will do that to you.

    I forgot to tell you about our social security miracle. After Ron's operation, I helped Ron apply for social security. This process started in March 2003. Ron was awarded the grant and received his first check in August 2003. Everyone I know that has applied for social security has waited years to obtain their first check.

During this process, I was also starting a home based business where I would assist businesses/individuals with investments. I also researched other Internet businesses. I met several clients via the Internet. I was skeptical but I informed them that I did not have money to invest and they would have to fund all of their investment transactions. I felt that when I told them this bit of information I would lose them as clients. I did not. As a matter of fact, they started to send checks to transact business, make investments for them. The first check I received was about $10,000. I went to my credit union to deposit it. They informed me that the funds would be on hold for 10 days. I then went to the bank that the check was drawn on, Affinity Credit Union. I then opened a checking and savings account. They also issued me a line of credit for overdraft protection. Here's some back ground information: the check was a cashier's bank check that was issued to Mary Wilson Butter. My name at that time was Mary

Wilson Butler. I informed the bank of my credit history which did not stop them from opening the account. I was to withdraw the money once it cleared and transfer funds to pay for fees and services to transfer my client's money into another account for investing. Even though the process of opening the account was positive, I was still skeptical but I felt that the bank would check to see that the check was good. The following morning, I went to the bank to withdraw the funds and the check had cleared. I then felt at ease and that all was fine. I went to my credit union and sent the funds via Western Union. There was a problem; I was not given a control number so the individuals I transferred it to could not receive it. I finally obtained the information needed to retrieve the funds. Through the whole process I was getting warnings. I was warned about transferring money to Africa. But this was my client's money and I was only doing as they directed. This transaction was finally successful. I was then sent another check and the same procedure was required. I sent the money via a Western Union center instead of my credit union. Before the funds were transferred, Western Union called and asked if I was sure about sending the money. Again I said yes because I felt the checks were good and it was not my money to question how the client wanted it distributed. I also received checks from other clients that valued over $10,000. These checks were not cashier checks so the bank waited five days for them to clear. I waited and they cleared. I transferred the funds to pay for services for my clients. These types of transactions occurred several more times with checks in varying amounts. One of the last checks I received was in the amount of $197,000, which also cleared. I had never seen a check that large nor had access to that amount for me to personally control. From the fee I charged my clients, I gave my church a check for $5000, bought clothes for Ron, paid bills and bought other necessities. Majority of the funds were to be transferred to another account. Affinity was able to perform this transaction. After transferring the $100K into the stated account, I received information from Mr. Thomson, my client, to stop payment and transfer funds to a different account. I asked the bank to perform this service. They said that they would attempt to stop payment but could not guarantee it.

On April 2nd I received a phone call from a man stating that he was from the Federal Reserve and that the check I deposited was counterfeit. I asked him for more information about the check and he could not give me the correct information. I then called my bank and told them of the strange phone call I received and told them not to send the funds until they verified the validity of the check. I received another check from one of my clients that same day. When I went to deposit it I learned that the check was counterfeit. The bank manager asked me if the other checks were good. I told them yes because I felt that the bank had checked out the checks before releasing funds. However I learned that all the checks were counterfeit. The bank froze my account. I called my Pastor and told him not to deposit the $5000 check and explained the situation to him. I gave the bank information about the checks I received. The bank told me that they would be contacting the authorities. A detective informed me that I was a victim of a scam that the FBI was investigating. I received a call from the FBI and made an appointment to bring all data I had to their office located in downtown Minneapolis, one block from my apartment. On April 8,

2003, I went to the FBI office and gave them all documentation from the transactions I had with my clients. I told them that I was still being contacted by my clients and I asked them how I should proceed. I was directed to inform my clients that I've been busy with my husband and that his health had turned worst. I sent them an email stating the above but I still received calls and threats about transferring the funds. The calls and emails finally stopped. I received a call from the FBI on April 25th stating that they would not prosecute me locally or federally but the bank may want to do a civil suit. The FBI informed me that they would make copies of my documents and forward them to the secret service. As of May 7, 2003, I have not heard from the bank nor has the freeze on my account been lifted. I finally received a statement from the bank that shows that I had a negative balance of $48,000. The bank did not call nor contact me about how I should rectify the negative balance. Then, Ron tells me that he knew something was wrong. I told him he did not seem to matter as long as I was buying things. But God helped us through this too.

Ron got better and wanted to drive the truck while I was at work. He went for drives; he said that he went to the Har-Mar Mall and walked around. I doubted him but God knew and I trust God.

I laugh at myself for the calm manner in which I give advice. My healing process was "gradual" but it seemed "endless" at the time I was going through it. The deliverance from fear of speaking and singing came as I obeyed God and entered into praise and worship of Him. I fully believe that God loves me all the time.

We can usually find another way to view our situation beyond how we initially see it. But when we walk in the light of the Lord, blessings abound for us in each moment. Sometimes, though, we have to deliberately look for them. God's light does not blind us, but we can be blind to God's light as I was for so many years. We don't always see the whole truth. Sometimes we see everything but the truth.

Learning to walk with God was difficult because I felt that I had no freedom. He wants us to take His hand, but He doesn't want us to let go. In fact, His desire is that we become more and more dependent upon Him for everything. I bought into the world's idea of independence. A deception Satan tries to enforce when you are trying to walk with God.

Remember how I like school and did quite well in it? Walking with God is like going to school. We are tested on the many things we learn. God's tests are not like the test taken in school. First of all, He already knows how much we know. The test is not for Him. It's for us. God's test helps us clearly see what we're made of. It teaches us about ourselves and about God. The test itself is part of our learning process.

The results of the tests God gives us, depending on our attitude in the midst of the testing, will determine whether we are refined like gold by the process or become cold and hard like steel. It won't necessarily be how much we know that counts, but what we do with the knowledge we've received. It's how we take the test.

In the test that God gives, we receive no grade. We will either pass, or we'll have to keep taking it until we do. We have two choices with regard to God's tests. We can resist God, have a bad attitude, and try to run from it. Or we can embrace Him in it and welcome His perfecting hand in our lives. Our reaction will determine the outcome.

Much of what God wants to work in us will come about as we grow in our relationships with the people God puts in our lives. Relationships can be difficult to navigate because of one major variable-the other person! Our darkest hours can come because of troubled times we have with people. Any kind of relationship can bring pain. That's because whether we want to acknowledge it or not, relationships are very important to each of us. We can't live without them. Nor were we ever intended to. Every relationship requires a sacrifice. Marriage, especially, has the greatest potential for deep emotional injury and by far the stiffest requirement for sacrifice. That's because the person who knows us best can hurt us most. If that was not so, we would not see such a high divorce rate.

In order to live life successfully in the present and move into the future God has planned for us, we have to step out of the past. If we don't, it will color everything we see and affect all we do. Keeping us in the past is another deception of Satan.

After the fraud incident, Ron and I grew closer. God gave him a revelation on how to love me. He testified to the church that he finally learned how to love his wife. I told him to sit back and watch the women try to test that love. I even told him who they would be. He later asked after the test; "how did you know that?" I told him that God gave me that information to pray about so I would not get upset by it and lose my peace.

I took Ron to his clinic appointments, preparing his medicine, taking his temperature, weighing him, and recording lab results in a book. His liver function started to return to normal levels. We were living and loving well. A day position opened at work so I could start attending church on Sunday. We were growing by leaps and bounds. Then the church members became jealous of our blessings and started rumors about us. We were hurt and angry. I wanted to leave the church. When a position opened in Chicago, I applied and was hired. Shell started to check out apartments I found via the net. Things were not moving as smoothly as we hoped. So, I asked Ron if he really wanted to move to Chicago and he said no. I had written a letter to our current apartment to be released from our lease and I accepted the job. I then asked God what to do. He told me to call my boss. I called my boss and told him that I no longer wanted the job and would like to return to my old position. Taking the job and moving to Chicago just did not feel right. My boss told me that he had never heard of anyone getting their old job back after accepting a new one. I told him, that if it's God's will for me to stay, he's going to see a miracle. I told him that I was going to pray and let God work it out. God did work it out; I was able to go back to my old position. Then God told me that we were to stay at the church because we had to learn something from this experience and to be a testimony to others. That hurt my flesh, but I was obedient. We started attending bible study at United Deliverance Temple, UDT, church in Minneapolis. We needed extra help through this time of testing. We became stronger. We started to believe that no weapon formed against us would prosper. Then Ron's liver functions numbers started to rise, which means his liver was deteriorating, and the Hepatitis C virus re-surfaced. The doctors started injecting him with interferon which made him very ill. Even though he was ill, he did not miss church. He then started bleeding from his rectum. We learned that a rupture in his colon was causing the bleeding. I would take him to the emergency room at the University of Minnesota Medical Center and they would admit him. He was prescribed more medication. They even added a blood pressure pill to aid in stopping the ruptures in his colon.

While I was at work, Ron would take drives to sit by the river. One day he told me that he had gotten lost. He also told me that his vision would go out, like a white out in a snow storm. I prayed to God, about how to get his truck keys without causing a scene. An opportunity became available when Ron laid his keys on the end table and went to the bath room. I removed the keys from the ring. The next day when he was preparing to go for a drive, he noticed that the keys were gone. He was upset but he realized that he should not be driving. He could have harmed himself or someone else. Now that Ron was not driving I had to drive everywhere.

Visits to the emergency room were becoming more frequent. On one occasion, he was not able to urinate. He was told, after being admitted and tested, that his kidneys and liver stopped functioning and that he needed to have dialysis to clean his blood. He asked me what he should do. I know he was tired of all the invasive procedures. I told him that it was up to him. I took him outside in a wheelchair and we both cried. Then God put a song on our hearts and we started to sing.

Ron was again on the transplant list. I started fasting and praying for a liver or healing, what ever God's will was for Ron. Twice we had close calls. I still did not miss a day of work even though I drove him to his appointments.

But I started to get tired. My patience was thinning. I kept praying for his healing. The Holy Spirit told me to stop trying to be superwoman. I finally asked for help. I asked a guy at church to drive Ron to dialysis and I would pick him up. Then I found Ron a ride from the American Cancer Society. I also started delivery of Meals on Wheels, so he would not try to cook while I was at work. Ron was weak; he would drop plates, pots, and glasses. Then he stopped eating the food from Meals on Wheels. So, I would come home from work, cook or go out to buy him something that he would eat. Since he was in the apartment all day, he wanted to go out too. I would take him for a drive.

Ron became weaker. He lost a lot of weight. When his body was not retaining water; his 6'2" frame was basically skin and bones. I started going to a counselor to have someone on earth to talk to. My primary care doctor prescribed an antidepressant. During this time I was concerned about my health and how my weight was affecting it. I also wanted some assistance with losing weight. I was told by my doctor that the antidepressants worked as an appetite suppressant.

The routine that kept me going through this time was, getting up early, praying, then exercising, and then going to work. Upon returning home, I would cook and/or take Ron for a drive or pick him up from dialysis. Several nights during the week I would attend bible study. Ron would accompany me if he felt up to it. The word of God was my strength. One day, we went to MaCarron's Lake, located on Rice St in St Paul, to talk. Ron told me that he was tired. I told him that if he wanted to go home, it would be ok. He said "no, I want to talk". I told him I was referring to going home to Jesus. We understood each other. He was at peace after having this talk. I then changed what I was praying for. I asked God to help me to deal with what was going to happen to Ron's life and to keep me strong. God is faithful and always does what's best for your life.

On the first Sunday in September, Ron was again not feeling very well, but I had to attend church to direct the choir and sing the sermonic solo. When I returned home, he was still laying in bed. He was bleeding from his rectum again but did not want to go to the hospital. He was not eating either. I took him for a drive and we returned home to rest. He got up to go the bathroom and almost fell down. Thank God for the chair we had in the hallway to aid in catching him. He wanted to be independent up to the end. He also only wanted me caring for him and he did not want his family to know of his condition. Remember, he still had issues about them not allowing him to stay with them when we were in Mississippi. All Sunday night until Monday morning, Ron was getting up, going to the bathroom, and bleeding from his rectum. He was still unable to release urine. I would awaken every time he got up. He had a dialysis appointment scheduled for Monday and a member of the American Cancer Society was scheduled to drive him to this appointment. The Holy Spirit told me to stay home because he was too weak to go and that I would have to call an ambulance to take him. I called into work for my first day off. I told Ron that I was going to take him to the hospital. He said, "Let me rest for a little while". I laid back down. He then gets up again to go to the bathroom. I tried to help him and he gets upset with me. He laid down on the couch and said that he could not breathe. I told him that I was going to call the ambulance. I started to get dressed. When I came out of the bathroom, Ron's eyes were open but he was not breathing. I started to shake him and yelled "you promised you would not leave me". I saw Ron's spirit return to his body. I dressed him and let the ambulance attendant into the apartment. They put him on the stretcher and took him to the elevator. He was staring at me the entire time. He did not talk. The elevator took us up to the top floor and then stopped on every floor on the way down. I asked the paramedics why they did not lock the elevator. They said they did not have a key. The paramedics asked if I wanted to ride in the ambulance and I told them no, that I would meet them at the University of Minnesota Medical Center (UMC). I drove to UMC and waited for Ron. The paramedics called UMC and told the ER staff that Ron could not make it to UMC so they took him to Hennepin County Medical Center (HCMC). I went ballistic. The ER workers were concerned if I could drive to the HCMC. I did it, after praying, but I don't remember how. Once I arrived at the hospital I was told that Ron had gone into cardiac arrest and they did not think he could make it to UMC. I was told that blood had accumulated around his heart making it difficult for him to breathe. The doctors had to drain the blood and re-start his heart. I was put into a waiting area and the Chaplain came to talk to me and told me that he would give me all the information he could get from Ron's team. I started to pray and phoned people to inform them of Ron's condition. I called the Pastor, my boss, and Sis Nina. Sis Nina came to the hospital in her wheel chair. I asked her to call my sister Natalie who was then to call Ron's family.

The doctor's told me that they were doing all they could and that they were performing a juggling act. They said that if things did not improve, they would ask me to make a decision to disconnect him from life support. Ron was not conscience or breathing on his own. His body started to swell because of water retention caused by his kidney failure and he was bleeding internally and from his nose. He did not look like the man I knew.

Ron's sister came to town and stayed at the hospital with him while I went to work. I kept going to work because I had put Ron in God's hand. There was nothing more I could do for him. Ron's sister would come to the apartment to bathe and return to the hospital to sit with Ron when the doctors were not working on him. Thank God for his comfort and the ability to comfort others. On Friday Sept 10, 2004, the doctors, called me at work to get permission to disconnect Ron from life support. At this moment, the Lord must have thought I could take on more. I've learned that God has his own way of preparing His soldiers. He gradually takes away things so that you have to stand on your own with Him. You can't keep depending on other people to be there. Consequently, pretty soon you have to depend solely upon Him. I was dependent upon a lot of people, to the degree that was unhealthy. I was deceived into thinking that I needed them.

So God said, "Okay, these people are starting to mean just a little too much to you, and I need you to move forward. Now watch this…"

So people started dying or stopped talking to me. The question for me was; what was I going to do?

After the call from the hospital, I left work, walked home to get my truck, and headed to the hospital. Upon arrival to the hospital, I called Pastor and waited for him to arrive before allowing the doctors to disconnect Ron. The doctors disconnect Ron from the machines and as he breathed his last breath, his sister goes wild. I was surprised I remained calm. I was on antidepressants, but they were not enough to bring the peace I felt. Ron's sister asked if I could send his body to Mississippi. I told her that I could not afford to do that. I told her that I could not afford to bury him and that God would have to provide. The Pastor informed me of a funeral director who then told me about applying for burial assistance from Hennepin County. My daughter and sister, Natalie, came to Minnesota for support. My apartment complex had suites available to rent on a daily basis for family and friends. The church paid for my family to stay in the apartment suites. I lived in a one bedroom apartment and Ron's sister stayed with me.

I completed and submitted the application for assistance to Hennepin County on Friday morning and was awarded the funds by the afternoon. Then I asked the Pastor if we could have the service on Monday. The Friday of Ron's death, I attended prayer and choir rehearsal. The Saturday night before the service, Natalie and I typed the obituary into the computer. We lost it several times but were able to print it, take it to Kinko's for pick up on Sunday. This same type of incident occurred when I was typing my mother's obituary. It was as if the spirit did not want it to be completed. Natalie loaned me the money for the obituaries. I gave Ron's shoes and clothes to his sister for his children. She asked me to take her to UPS and she mailed the items to her home in Mississippi. She never offered to help with any of the service arrangements. Ron was cremated. I did not want to see him dead again and it was also cheaper. On Sunday, my daughter, sister, and Ron's sister accompanied me to church. I sang and directed the choir, something neither of them had seen me do. They were pleasantly surprised. On Monday, the day of Ron's service, God gave me the strength to console others as a way to help me to make it through. The service was a nice homecoming for Ron. His sister was very grief stricken. I guess that was to be expected, she had not had very much contact with him until we paid her the money Ron borrowed. Remember, when we were in Mississippi, Ron's family would not allow him to stay with them. He was hurt by this and only spoke to them after paying his sister the money he borrowed years earlier. I attributed my calmness to God and the fact that I know I did what I was suppose to do for Ron. Plus, I was on antidepressants. I returned to work the following Monday.

A Safety Information Specialist position with my company became available. I applied and interviewed. I was then offered the position. I went to New York for training. The position paid more than Ron's social security check and my former salary combined. Even though I lost him and had no insurance to bury him, God provided to pay the bills.

I was still attending Berean, directing the choirs, giving a message on children's Sunday, MC, singing sermonic solos, and attending school. I was also attending several bible studies, one at

Greater Faith Christian Center, GFCC. I still attended United Deliverance Temple, UDT's and Berean's bible study. I prayed to become closer to God. God told me to stop taking the antidepressants and learn to trust Him more. By July 2005, I stopped taking the antidepressants. I was driving back from Chicago, after the 4th of July weekend, and grief hit me like a ton of bricks. I was crying and could not understand why I felt badly. I went to my doctor to get a check up. I was having chest pains, head, and muscle aches. The doctor did not find anything. The Holy Spirit told me to read the booklet I received from HCMC on grief. After reading the booklet, I discovered that I was only grieving. I went to the bible and received a scripture that helped me through this process. I came upon Matt 5:4, blessed are they that mourn, for they shall be comforted.

I stood on this promise and every time I started to cry I would quote that scripture and I would be comforted. The Holy Spirit also told me to stop attending all the bible studies and grieve. I dropped all but the bible study at Berean. I was also praying for a new start in life. I became discouraged about attending Berean. I kept attending and performing my duties but I was also praying for deliverance. I spoke to the Pastor about decreasing my duties and stated that after Thanksgiving we would talk about which duties I would eliminate. I again started attending GFCC bible study. I felt this is where I was suppose to be but did not know how to get out of my obligations at Berean. After Thanksgiving, when I returned to talk to the Pastor about which duties I would perform, he told me that he arranged for the piano player to be president of the choir and for his nephew to direct. I was shocked but later realized that God had moved the obstacles out of my way so I could start a new life. That Sunday I joined GFCC. I went through new members classes. I was appointed praise team leader and I joined the prayer team.

I met a man who was becoming a good friend. We talked and joked a lot. He would tell me that he loved my spirit. I knew he liked me but I was not looking for a husband. One day, after a message he preached, I got his telephone number from a sister at church. I called him and we talked and laughed for hours. I thought this is what I was looking for in a friendship, for again, I was not looking for a husband.

God had been my husband and providing for all my needs per God's revelation to me from Isaiah 54. I told Mitchell about my past and he continued to talk to me.

One day, Mitchell informed me that God told him to ask for my hand in marriage. I told him that I needed to pray about it. I prayed, and started crying because I got an answer that I did not want to hear. The Holy Spirit told me to get my bible. I looked at a list of qualifications, I wrote in my bible of the type of husband I wanted. I wrote this before Ron and I married. As I read those traits, I felt that Mitchell was sent by God. God also told me to wait six months. I told him yes and set a date for six months away. I told him that God was healing some things in me. Later we both went before the Lord and were given permission to marry sooner, at least that's what I thought. The Pastor of GFCC also encouraged us to marry sooner. The Pastor also told us that we did not need counseling because we were mature Christians. We were married on April 15, 2006. We both were ordained Assistant Pastors the following weekend. God was blessing us. I tell you all this to let you see that God has bought me out of the darkness of drugs and sexual immorality and promoted me. Galatians 6: 7-9 "do not be deceived: God cannot be mocked. A man reaps what he sows. The one who sows to please his sinful nature, from that nature will reap destruction; the one who sows to please the Spirit, from the Spirit will reap eternal life. Let us not become weary in doing well, for at the proper time we will reap a harvest if we do not give up".

I thought all was well; we consummated our marriage on the wedding night. On April 27th I wrote the follow email to the Pastor of GFCC about an incident that occurred on the 26th.

Pastors, when we arrived home I told Mitchell that I was hurt, because I felt that he was not concerned about my needs, not providing for my needs. He felt that he provided for my needs when he cooked one night this week. That was not the issue; I felt that I did not matter. We were the last people to leave the church last night. I know there are certain duties that an Asst Pastor is suppose to perform, but I am an Asst Pastor too. In the truck, on the way home, Mitchell made a joke, but at the time he said it, I did not know that he was joking. He said, "you could be doing something too, you are an Asst Pastor". I told him that I was talking to people and he told me that I was socializing. That was the joke. I feel as Asst Pastors we are to help the Pastor but not to a detriment of our own marriage. If I am to be an Asst Pastor, beyond just in name, I must take on some of the duties that Mitchell has so he does not have to carry the full load and we can arrive home at a decent hour. I wake up early in the morning, around 0430. I need to be in bed by 0930 but I stay up and spend time with him. He does not have to get up until he's ready. He can handle most of his business at home. If he gets tired he can lay down. He does not have to put on his clothes if he doesn't want to. I came to this marriage knowing that I would be taking care of the house/finances until his business started to generate income. That is not the issue; the issue is consideration of me. One has to take care of home. Yes, God is first but he ordained families and they must be taken care of, God first, family and then man. He told me that I was full of the devil and that I did not know what I was talking about. I feel he socializes and handles other business besides church business too. I know this all takes time. I don't want him to stop being helpful, I just want consideration for me and my time. I feel that **everybody** comes *before me. I came home from work, cooked dinner and then went to bible study. I asked him to take the meat out for me to cook, and he only took out half of it, and his excuse was that he was on both phones. I let that go. You know, you have to choose your battles.*

The first time I saw this behavior was when I brought the papers for you to sign before we were married. He was sitting down talking to a sister and you said, "come here and sign these papers", he took his time coming, finished talking to the sister and then came. You then said, "this should be handled first and that sister could wait". He has done similar things on other occasions too. I did not address them when it happened because I was being considerate of his time, and thought that was what I was suppose to do, thinking that I would reap what I sow. What I am reaping is not what I sowed. If I am wrong in my thinking, feel free to point me in the right direction. This week was very stressful for me. I've had something planned everyday after work. He knew this and he still did not think, "I better get Mary home so she can get some rest for tomorrow". It was as if my needs were not important to him. Being tired is one of my triggers. I cannot be too hungry, angry, lonely, or tired. HALT. If this happens I'm in danger of not being very godly. I've informed him of this so that this does not cause problems for us. He constantly pushes that tired button. Even Jesus rested. Am I supposed to push myself more? How do I disconnect the tired button? I can only do so much. I know we are to speak, I can do all things through Christ who strengthens me, but my body don't always agree.

Love

Mary

Mitchell told me that the Pastors thought differently of me since I wrote the email and I should not have gone to them.

I got a check in my spirit when we applied for our marriage license; we were informed that the fee would be less if we participated in counseling and provided documentation. The Pastor signed the form stating that we received counseling when we did not. Mitchell agreed. Before these incidents I felt uncomfortable but I just pushed it aside. After we were married that feeling did not go away, it increased. I kept hearing, tell the truth and shame the devil; this was Ron's, my second husband who passed away, saying. But I did not heed that warning. Mitchell worked his business at home and he expected me to cook when I arrived home. He did cook occasionally but not as often as I. Then he started to complain about my contentious spirit. I prayed to God, for help to be the best wife I could; to change me. But I still felt uncomfortable. He complained about my snoring. I purchased Breathe-Right Strips and throat spray. Then he started talking about the bed being uncomfortable and not sleeping with me. He would sleep on the couch. He told me that his back was bothering him. The couch was a futon and it was not as comfortable as the bed. I reminded him that he said that the bed was comfortable, and asked what changed? He said that he did not know. When that excuse was not accepted he then said that I was a big woman and that he did not have enough room to sleep in the bed. I then told him that he was aware of my size before we married, so that excuse was also not acceptable. I also reminded him that he said that he enjoyed sex and wanted it often. (I later learned after finding his journal, when he moved out, that he claimed to be a sex addict) I asked that he be honest with me. He was not. I told him that I was not going to live in a loveless marriage. I reminded him that I was once married to a man who wanted to stay married to hide his sexual preference.

During our marriage, Mitchell and the Pastor talked on the telephone every day. They would go out to eat every Thursday. Before we married the Pastor asked that I allow Mitchell to continue their weekly dinner engagement. I saw nothing wrong with that, at the time. Remember, the email I wrote to the Pastor about the communication problems Mitchell and I were having, and Mitchell getting upset and told me that the Pastor thinks differently of me? I also told Mitchell that I should be able to talk to the Pastor without being judged, but that was just another red flag for me.

I informed Mitchell that he would have to leave. He asked for grace to find an apartment. I said yes. We had this conversation on Sunday June 11, 2006. When I returned home from work on June 12, 2006, Mitchell was moving his things from the apartment. While at work, I was getting a strong urge to start the divorce process. I went to Hennepin County's website and started completing the summons and dissolution of marriage forms. I had them notarized and bought them home. As Mitchell were moving his things out of the apartment. I said, "I have something else for you to take with you", and gave him the summons and asked that he sign the paper stating that he received it. He was in total shock. He looked at the date and stated, "I'm not signing anything". I said "ok, you don't have to do anything". He packed a few more items and left. Before he left I asked for the keys. He said that he would be returning to get the remainder of his belongings on Thursday of that week. When he returned on Thursday he bought two guys from the church to help. These incidents were not the only causes that led to our break-up. Mitchell's business was not producing income. He borrowed money from one of his friends to pay his car note. He could not deposit those funds into his bank because he had been writing checks without depositing money into his account. I had an extra saving account that I allowed him to deposit the funds. The finance company withdrew the money from that account. When the next payment was due they again tried to withdraw the funds. Thank God, my credit union called to ask if I wanted the transaction paid. I told them no and told Mitchell about the finance company attempt. Of course, a fee was charged to my account. I asked Mitchell to cover it and he said that he would when he got some money. My financial situation became very shaky; I was, again, taking care of a man. I was short for my car note because of the fees charged to the account. I told Mitchell about it. He told me to pray as he did and God will provide. I did just that and God made it possible for me to obtain a new car. I bought a 2006 Honda Element. I always wanted that vehicle but I tried to please my man and purchased what they wanted.

The Pastors of GFCC did not call us to come in for counseling, remember, we were Assistant Pastors. The members were even forbidden to speak to me. Those who did were pressured to stop and eventually asked to leave the church. This is just more confirmation.

Mitchell never changed his mailing address to his new place of residence. I kept receiving mail and phone calls from his bill collectors. I learned that Mitchell was still writing bad checks for gas and other items. Then the finance company gained possession of his car. He was able to convince someone to lease him a car and he stopped paying for it. They were looking for their money and the car too. Mitchell wanted me to send his mail to him instead of changing his mailing address, which would aid in the bill collectors not finding him. I would tell the bill collectors that Mitchell did not live with me and I gave them his last known address.

After Mitchell left, I called the Pastor of Berean church and told him of my situation and asked if I could return. I was not looking for a position but a place to worship. He said that he knew the marriage and the church was not going to work for me. He also said that I was not ready to hear that. Even though I may not have been ready to hear it, I wish someone would have said something about the decision I made. The Pastor said I could return. Not much had changed since I left. Some new faces but still the same spirit. I also graduated from Bible school and the Pastor of Berean did not recommend me for Missionary or any other title at that time. God told me that He gives promotion not man. If this had happened to me when I was living in sin, I would have turned to drugs and sex for comfort. As you can see I depended on God. He has been my ever present help in my times of need. Even though people in the church hurt me, I was not going to allow them to turn me away from God.

On June 15, 2006, I was still in the divorce process. I notified Mitchell via publication. I also started a new job as a Capital Planner, where I manage million dollar budgets. I started to search for a new home which I could possible rent with option to buy. The home I was interested in was no longer available. I was informed of another location in Lino Lakes. The agent on site was not familiar with the rent with option to buy program. I thought to myself, Lino Lakes is too far from work. In late June, I went to see the home after work. The drive from work was not bad in spite of the construction. I toured the models and liked what I saw. The sales agent informed me that the model was for sale. I asked her, "How do I apply?" She told me to fill out the application and pay $500 earnest money to hold it. I forgot to tell you that Mitchell wanted us to buy a home too. He went to one of his friends and got us pre-approved. He had no money so I would have to provide everything. I just thank God for the transaction not working with him. Now, back to the story, I completed the application and put it in God's hand. Did you know when a model is sold; all of the furniture comes with it? Also remember, my credit was not the best from the foreclosure and the bankruptcy on my credit report. But with God all things are possible. I was approved and a closing date was set. My divorce was finalized on September 13th. I closed on September 22nd. Without God this would never have happened. I received a 6.25% fixed interest rate, a full house of furniture, and the remainder of the lease, on the apartment I lived in, paid in full so I could move before the end of my lease. As I was planning my move and changing my address I also completed a change of address card for Mitchell after calling his cell phone to confirm his address. I moved many of my things myself. Judy, a lady from work, and her husband helped me move the heavy stuff. The other items, my old bed, table, microwave oven, dishes, piano, and futon that were left in the apartment I sold for less than $50. No one from Berean helped, even though they said they would. Sometimes God blocks people you depend on for help so you can see His hand in your situation. That was fine, God get's all the credit, He arranged for everything.

These past few years of strengthening my relationship with God were a surprise to see how I have gotten closer to who I am and who He wants me to be. I am free from Satan's web of deception. I am quite happy seeing myself through God's eyes.

We all come to self-knowledge in different ways and at different times. Sure I wish I could have been smarter when I was younger, and then again, I know women my age and older who still haven't figured this out. Can they be judged or criticized? No more than anybody else and especially not by me. I may be the last person, who can give any advice about anything, but I am willing to share the little that I've learned, and it's an ongoing process.

It's all about choices. The only choice we don't make is to wake up; God makes that one for us. The remainder of the day is a banquet of choices to choose from. You can choose how you will use the world around you. But the trick is also how you let the world use you.

Where am I now in my life? Well, I know that God knows best what I need-better than I ever could. But I have to stop fighting Him and obey. There is a saying that goes, "Get out of God's way and into the word… and don't block your blessing!"

I have recently been appointed to the position of Evangelist. This is not to say that now I'm doing everything right, far from it. I still may not be what I ought to be, but thank the Lord; I'm not what I used to be.

My life is a journey that has covered a lot of ground. If your own life is filled with hills, valleys, and deserts, count it all joy. All you have to do is keep on livin' to know that eventually life will kick your behind and knock you down. It's your job to get back up and kick back. Character is born when you're tested, so when you are tested, know that God is trying to tell you something.

It's tempting to put your tail between your legs and run for the hills. Or you can always hide your head in the sand with your backside sticking out. Or you can change your name to "It-Wasn't-Me-I-Didn't-Do-It-Leave-Me-Alone" and live in denial. The choices are many. You can choose to live a life that is bitter, or better. You will either find solace in the medicine cabinet, the neighborhood bar, or some other mood-altering substance. A negative outlook eventually takes its toll on your relationships, your health, and everything else you hold dear.

I guess what I am trying to pass on to you, dear reader, is this; don't give up…God ain't through with you yet.

There's a scripture in the bible that reads: "To whom much is given, much is required." If you only focus on what you don't have, you are missing out on so much more. If you're too consumed with what others may have, be careful. You don't know what goes on behind closed doors. They may only seem to have it all together, but they also may be going through hell when nobody is looking. And don't discount someone who seems not to have very much at all, that same person might be the one who saves your life.

Do I have regrets? I think that's a bad question, but I would say yes- and no. I could never have become the woman I am today without each and every experience I've gone through. There were times I put myself in the fire, and there were times that God put me in the fire. Both times He brought me through it. For every negative, there was a positive. For every dark passage, I was ultimately led to the light. I appreciate the pleasure, because I've had the pain. That's the way it is. There is no victory without the battle.

If you know Christ, you will not be deceived. Jesus is the way, the truth, and the light. Who the Son sets free is free indeed. Jesus came to destroy the deceptive practices of Satan and all who is used by him. God is faithful, and His word is true. God does not love me more than He loves you. If He did it for me, He will do it for you too, if you only believe and let Him.

I Would Like to Hear From You

If you have a testimony to share after reading this book, please send an email to MaryTaylor@MaryTaylorsite.com or MaryTaylor@DeceptiontotheNthDegree.com or visit the site www.DeceptiontotheNthDegree.com

Also available from Mary Taylor

Thus Saith the Lord

Inspiration from God

Bibliography

Scripture reference from the King James Version of <u>The Holy Bible</u>

Ellis, Millicent F., Evangelist, <u>Harvest Readiness Manual Part I.</u> N.p.: founder of Love, Faith and Hope Ministries (1-11)

www.ingramcontent.com/pod-product-compliance
Lightning Source LLC
Chambersburg PA
CBHW031628160426
43196CB00006B/327